HOW **W** COMPL

HOW YOU CAN WIN COMPETITIONS

ENTERING & WINNING CONSUMER COMPETITIONS

Elizabeth Simpson

JAVELIN BOOKS

LONDON · NEW YORK · SYDNEY

First published in the UK 1988 by Javelin Books, an imprint of Cassell plc,
Artillery House, Artillery Row, London SW1P 1RT

Copyright © 1988 Elizabeth Simpson

Distributed in the United States by
Sterling Publishing Co., Inc.,
2 Park Avenue, New York, NY 10016

Distributed in Australia by
Capricorn Link (Australia) Pty Ltd,
PO Box 665, Lane Cove, NSW 2066

Simpson, Elizabeth
  How you can win competitions: entering
  and winning consumer competitons.
  1. Competitions
  I. Title
  790.1'34

ISBN 0-7137-2057-3

Typeset by St. George Typesetting, Redruth, Cornwall
Printed and bound in Great Britain by Cox & Wyman Ltd., Reading, Berks.

CONTENTS

ABOUT THE AUTHOR

Like most of us Elizabeth Simpson was hardly ever excited by what the postman pushed through her letter-box – either bills or junk mail. That was before she discovered 'comping'. In January of her first year of entering, Elizabeth received her first letter of congratulations, as prize-winner in a Kitchens Competition, and by March of that year was the delighted owner of a luxury fitted kitchen. Now bitten by the 'comping' bug, Elizabeth began to enter competitions regularly and devised a system to ensure no closing dates passed unnoticed and no entry form was lost. That system netted Elizabeth prizes worth over £6,000 in her first year of 'comping' and she entered her second full of confidence, having won £700 worth of prizes in January alone.

Married, with two youngsters aged 5 and 3 years, Elizabeth finds that her lucrative hobby fits into whatever spare time she can devote to it. But more importantly it provides the challenging pastime she was looking for to exercise those 'little grey cells' untaxed by home chores and the chatter of children.

Elizabeth maintains that she is not a 'lucky person' and that anyone who reads her light-hearted but comprehensive book can match, if not surpass, her own successes.

ACKNOWLEDGEMENTS

Many thanks to Paul and Mark Samways.

INTRODUCTION

There is no aura of mystery about winning competitions. The people who do are just like you or me. Take me, for example. I've won prizes valued at over £6,000 in only seven months of 'comping'. And there is absolutely no reason why *you* can't do the same.

Like you probably do now, I used to believe that the 'winners' in life were simply 'lucky' people. I couldn't explain *why* they were luckier than me; I just knew that I never won anything. In fact, it's amazing how common the notion is that prize-winners are 'lucky', rather than sensible, methodical people who take a professional approach to, and enjoy, entering competitions. But then I sat down and thought about it: I never *entered* any competitions, so how could I expect to win prizes?

Many people, who have been astounded by (and envious of) my success, say to me: 'It's not fair, I never win anything'. My reply is always the same: 'But do you ever enter competitions? No? Well, then you can't honestly expect to win, can you?'

That's what this book is all about: to show you that once you start to enter competitions regularly, *there is absolutely no reason* why that brand-new car, kitchen, holiday or even money can not be yours.

Ever since the mid-nineteenth century, when consumer and magazine competitions were first thought of, products have appeared on counters and shelves offering many and varied inducements to buy them. These inducements have taken the form of money-off vouchers, free gifts, two-for-the-price-of-one and competitions. The most common big prizes currently on offer include cars, foreign holidays, time-share villas and money, but houses, kitchens, conservatories and DIY vouchers are fast heading a list which adds up to an Aladdin's cave of rewards for little more than the cost of an envelope and stamp.

All you have to do to share in this prize bonanza is to take the time to read this book, then put my advice into practice. Start the next time you visit the supermarket. Take the time to look – yes, really look – at all the products on offer. Examine any leaflets being given away free. Then when you have got together a few entry forms, use the information you can find in this book to help you complete each one. Keep searching for competitions each time you go out to buy something – it will soon become second nature to you – and you'll discover what fun 'comping' can become. Send in as many competitions each month as your budget will allow and keep this up *every month*. You'll soon find out what an absorbing, interesting hobby 'comping' is. Exciting too, for who knows, one of these days, quite soon, a big, white envelope congratulating you on your first win could drop through your letter-box.

Now read *how* you can begin to make it all happen.

CHAPTER 1

DE-MYSTIFYING
THE ART OF 'COMPING'

HOW I BECAME A SUCCESSFUL COMPER

I actually won my first competition 12 years ago – £100-worth of hairdressing appointments, and in those days £100 went a long way.

At that time I was in a fairly boring job with a lot of spare time on my hands; time I spent mostly reading magazines. As I had very little money to spend on luxuries, the magazines I looked at were usually the ones handed out free at London stations. For a bit of fun, and to relieve the boredom, I would enter every competition featured in those free magazines and one morning received a telegram from the publishers congratulating me on winning first prize in their 'Hair Knowledge' competition. Believe me, in the 12 months that my prize was valid, I had my hair changed in every way imaginable!

I might have entered the odd competition or two in the years that followed; I can't honestly remember. What I do know is that I never won anything – not even in a raffle-ticket draw!

Eventually, as a housewife making regular visits to my local supermarket, I started to pick up the odd competition entry form and realised how much satisfaction there was in visiting the local reference library for answers to the questions set. After a number of years bringing up two children, it was nice to exercise those 'little grey cells' again, and I was becoming quite knowledgeable about a whole variety of subjects. Competitions, I soon decided, would provide me with an interesting pastime; one that would cost very little to enjoy and which might – just might – reward me with the odd prize or two.

I'd read about 'professional compers' who won large numbers of valuable prizes each year by entering every competition they could lay their hands on. They *entered* lots of competitions and they were *successful*. It reminded me of the principle taught to new salesmen during my days working in sales and marketing, commonly called 'The Numbers Game': the greater the number of people you call on, the greater your chance of a sale. Or, to give another, more common analogy, the more mud that's thrown against the wall, the more that's likely to stick to it!

I soon realised that, as shown by my very first 'hairdressing' win, the more competitions I entered, the greater my chances of winning one of them. That, I decided, was the first lesson to learn if I was to become a successful 'comper' myself.

My first big competition win occurred in January 1987. I always buy a certain brand of breakfast cereal and had started to collect the tokens needed for entering their kitchen competition. Usually I would throw the empty packet away without clipping off the tokens, or I'd put the tokens in a drawer and forget all about them until it was too late to enter – does that sound familiar to you? However, as we had just moved into a house which had a badly designed kitchen with old, rather grubby, units, the prospect of winning a brand-new one certainly appealed to me.

Once I'd collected the maximum number of tokens, I was entitled to eight lines in this 'order-of-merit' competition (which is covered fully in Chapter 4). I had to rearrange eight reasons for choosing a new kitchen in the correct order of importance and, as a tie-breaker, suggest one additional reason myself.

To be honest, the last two or three lines were filled in rather haphazardly – I had almost missed the competition closing date and wanted to get my entry sent off as quickly as possible.

Four months passed and I had completely forgotten about this competition, when I received a white envelope in the post one Saturday morning. Imagine my delight when I read that I was one of only five winners nation-wide who would receive a brand-new kitchen, delivered and fitted absolutely free. My prize included a new washing-machine, dishwasher, fan oven and built-in fridge and freezer. Believe me, to receive that letter was a wonderful experience, and one which taught me a second, valuable lesson in successful 'comping'. In future I would have to be more *organised* – I nearly didn't win because I had almost left it too late to enter.

Boosted by this wonderful success, I began to enter every competition I came across and within four months had won the following prizes: gold jewellery; camera equipment; champagne dinner for two at a top French restaurant; silk lingerie; a steam press (valued at over £300); and a colour TV.

Since then, hardly has a month gone by without the news of yet another prize – often two or more.

As I entered more and more competitions, I began to devise a system which I'm now passing on to you. I can't guarantee you instant success; after all, no one can hope to win *every* competition they enter. All I can say is that my methodical and regular approach to comping has helped me win all these prizes, and more, and it can do so for you as well.

WHAT PREVENTS PEOPLE FROM ENTERING COMPETITIONS?

The biggest reason, I suppose, for the large numbers of people who don't enter competitions is disinterest. I can't understand why, but presumably the thought of winning some of the thousands of prizes on offer each year holds no allure for some people. I shall not try to convince the disinterested that comping is for them as you are unlikely to fit into that category. After all, you must have some measure of interest, otherwise you wouldn't have bought or borrowed this book?

Let's look instead at some of the other groups of people who never enter, and therefore never win, competitions – which one do you belong to?

The Sceptics

When I announced to my friends and family that I had won a luxury fitted kitchen, it was amazing how many of them were convinced that there was a 'catch'. The greatest sceptics among them informed me (where they got such knowledge from, I don't know!) that at worst, I would be expected to pay towards some of the work and, at best, I would have little or no choice on the design of the units offered. I tried to answer those points as positively as possible, saying that the companies involved in promoting the competition were reputable, national manufacturers who were unlikely to want their good names and reputations attached to anything which might be considered underhand. However, with no past experience of winning such a large competition prize, I must admit that I was a little worried about all these remarks.

The reality was, thankfully, completely opposite to what the sceptics had expected. Not only did I have a completely free choice of the type of units I could choose, but I was

14

involved in all stages of the planning of the kitchen. The only thing not included in the price of it all was the cost of redecorating afterwards. This we had intended to do anyway, and the cost of that was less than £200. Considering the additional value that the kitchen had given to our house, we considered ourselves very well done by, indeed!

Not to be outdone, the sceptics then announced that I would be expected to undertake all kinds of never-ending publicity in 'payment' for my prize. Well, there *was* a champagne reception arranged at a top hotel at which my husband and I were sole guests. The local Press were invited and I had my picture in a couple of newspapers. But that's where the publicity ended and I can't honestly say I wanted to resist quaffing endless champagne and eating canapés in such luxurious surroundings. After all, those 'Queen-for-a-day' occasions are few and far between.

This story goes some way to illustrate how wrong the sceptics are. Most competitions are run by reputable companies in order to promote their products and increase sales, and winners needn't worry that they are about to be hoodwinked in some way – they aren't. Some winners, even when they have won major prizes, are not required to be involved in any publicity at all and their prizes are posted to them. Some have even had cars driven to their homes and the keys deposited with them quite unceremoniously. Unless it has been written into the rules that the prize is conditional upon the winner agreeing to undertake a certain amount of publicity, no respectable company will force you into having your name published or picture taken if you don't want it. My husband was a little worried that, after our picture had appeared in the Press, we would be bombarded by salesmen trying to sell us insurance policies. We weren't – only the usual phone calls from companies trying to interest us in one of their kitchens!

You will notice that I used the words 'most competitions' in the above paragraph. I shall be drawing your attention, in Chapter 2, to a few competitions which I choose to avoid, and which I suggest you do too; but these amount to such a small fraction of the thousands of competitions advertised each year, that it's silly to ignore competitions altogether in order to avoid being 'conned' by the odd one or two. The advice I shall give you later will enable you to spot the less-than-straightforward competitions so that you can ignore them altogether.

The 'Negatives'

Since my own success at winning competitions, I've inspired (if that's the right word) some of my friends and relatives to have a go too. In fact, many were delighted simply to hear of someone who actually *won*. On the other hand, there were those who shrugged their shoulders, announcing that I was luckier, brighter, more able than they were. 'I can't answer the questions' or 'I can't write slogans' were the most common excuses. Well, why not? As I've said before, I'm no luckier than anyone else. After all, I haven't won a million pounds on the football pools – yet! I'm certainly no more intelligent than the majority of people I know. As to being more able, well, perhaps they are right with that one. I *do* have the ability to organise myself and to try to succeed in whatever course of action I choose. But such organisation and dedication are not my divine right – everyone can acquire them, with a little know-how. That's why I wrote this book, to show *you* – whether you find answers difficult to find, or slogans difficult to write – that for every competition there is a winner. Why not ensure that, very soon, that winner is *you*?

'I haven't got the time'

You go shopping, don't you? Once you've got into the habit, it doesn't take much more time to keep an eye open for competitions. Comping needn't be time-consuming. OK, you might need to spend the odd morning in the reference section of your library if you haven't got a good selection of reference books at home, but that can be a relaxing and rewarding experience in itself. And slogans can be thought of while preparing the children's tea or washing the car. Time doesn't have to be a problem. If you have the will to succeed, you'll always find the time. After all, I have two children under 6, run a small company from home, write short stories for publication, knit, sew, keep a large garden in order and *still* find the time to be a successful comper – so can you.

A LITTLE EFFORT GOES A LONG WAY

I know of no area of life in which there are rewards to be had for little or no effort. So it is with competitions. Unless you're prepared to look for answers and give some thought to the slogans you are asked to complete, then I'm afraid your chances of winning will be very slim indeed.

It's up to you how much effort you put into your hobby and how much you'll get out of it. But the beauty of comping is that it can fit into any life-style – from someone who works full time and can only fit it into their leisure hours, to a person working from home, like myself, who can look for inspiration at odd times in the day.

It's a perfect pastime for the retired, and certainly a lucrative one for those willing to approach it in a 'professional' way – and the following chapters will show you how.

From letters I've seen, written by regular compers across

the country, there are men and women, young and old, who never have to pay for an annual holiday, furnish their homes for free, give away Christmas presents they haven't had to pay for and even boost their bank balance with cash sums that the tax man can't get his hands on! They didn't meet with such success by only sending in the occasional entry form. They are regular compers who have increased their chances of winning by applying some thought, and a little hard work, to their entries. What I aim to show you in the following pages is how, by putting in the same degree of effort, you can have some fun and stack the odds in your favour too.

CHAPTER 2

HOW TO FIND
YOUR ENTRY FORMS

Just a quick word about the term 'competitions'. I have covered every type of *consumer* competition I've so far come across, which means those that are connected in some way with the purchase of goods – be it a can of food, a magazine or a piece of equipment for the home. Short-story or poetry competitions are not included. However, I have included one of the easiest and least time-consuming of all competitions – the prize draw. They generally require nothing more than filling in your name and address to which your prize can be forwarded. But more of that later. Let's now look at the best places to find all the wonderful consumer competitions on offer week after week.

THE MOST COMMON SOURCES OF COMPETITIONS

Supermarkets

A large proportion of competitions are found on the labels and wrappers of the vast number of consumer products on supermarket shelves. It could be a can of beans, a chocolate bar, washing-up liquid, cereal packet or cleaning fluid. In fact, virtually no product is exempt, even the makers of male contraceptives have been known to get in on the act!

So remember, someone somewhere is offering *you* the chance to win a prize.

Have a good, slow look at the supermarket shelves next time you're doing your weekly shopping. You'll be amazed at how many competitions can be found there.

Certain supermarket chains promote more competitions than others. Some, in addition to stocking products with national competitions on them, often team up with a particular manufacturer for a combined promotion, which means that the competition is only featured in their chain of stores.

That's why I don't restrict my shopping to one chain only, but vary my trips between the ones I know run the greatest number of competitions. If there are a few large stores in your area, why not try doing the same?

This is a good starting-point for newcomers to comping, as any type of competition run by just one chain of store often receives a lower number of entries than one run by a company promoting on-pack competitions in a wide variety of chains nationally. The questions set are generally very easy and, from what I've seen of the resulting winning slogans, the standard of entries remain firmly fixed in the 'I buy brand X because . . . my family like it.' mould. Offer something a bit different here and the odds are certainly in your favour!

Another reason why I vary my shopping expeditions is that I like to pick up a copy of the in-store magazines produced by some chains, such as Asda's *Hi-Time* and Gateway's *Goodtime* and *Freezertime*. These are available quarterly or monthly, although you'll have to check with your own local store as to when copies are available, as this can vary; but generally, the in-store magazines are distributed at the beginning of each month. Why am I interested in them? Because, among the adverts, editorial and money-off coupons, there is usually at least one competition – often two or three.

In addition to looking at the wrappers and getting a copy of the in-store magazine, try looking in the little perspex containers attached to the shelves of many stores. Sometimes they simply contain information about a certain product, sometimes a money-off coupon which can be useful. Mostly (and most important to me), they contain competition entry forms. Why not look out for them next time you are in a store?

Other Shops

Every shop, store, pub, newsagent, garage, garden centre – in fact anywhere you can *buy* something – is a potential source of competition entry forms. It's just a question of keeping your eyes open.

For example, my husband and I went shopping in a menswear shop recently. While he was paying for his purchases, I wandered around the displays and spotted a free in-store magazine. On one of the pages was a coupon for a free draw. The prize? A wonderful ski-ing holiday for two. This hadn't been generally advertised and I wouldn't have known about it if I hadn't taught myself *always* to look at in-store magazines. I filled in the coupon and had to hunt around for the box to put it in, but I eventually found it positioned on top of one of the displays. It didn't sound as if my entry was meeting many others on its way to the bottom! Perhaps few people bother to pick up this particular in-store magazine. If that's the case, they're unlikely to have seen the competition and what you don't see you can't enter. The fewer entrants there are, the better the chance for those who *do* enter – like me. After all, I haven't been ski-ing for years . . . Make sure you're in with that chance too.

Chemists' shops are a good source of competitions, particularly the bigger ones. Again, look out for leaflets attached to the shelves and 'collars' attached to products, such as sun-tan lotion, shampoo, conditioner and hairspray. Next time you need to buy batteries or video tapes, why not have a good look at all the different brands (there often isn't much difference price-wise) to see if one of them is promoting a competition?

Off-licences periodically produce free news-sheets in which they feature their own competitions. On their shelves they stock various brands of wines, spirits and beers which, at some time or another throughout the year, will run a competition. Take your time choosing a replacement for your drinks' cabinet. By varying your choice each time, to take advantage of any competitions which are being featured, you're taking an important step towards winning a valuable prize.

Holidays are a favourite prize of drinks' manufacturers, the destination for which is usually related to the place of origin of the product concerned – France for French wine for example. If you fancy winning a holiday and regularly purchase from an off-licence, keep your eyes open for the 'collars' on the necks of bottles. They signal competitions, and competitions mean *prizes*!

Magazines and Newspapers

If you buy magazines regularly, you'll have, no doubt, noticed that some contain competitions in every issue. Weeklies, like *Weekend* have several competitions featured in each issue, offering small prizes like games, cameras or LPs. The monthlies, such as *She* or *Family Circle*, run competitions with bigger prizes, like cars or holidays. In fact, you'll hardly find a month goes by without at least one

22

competition to enter in the popular women's weeklies or monthly magazines.

TV Times and *Radio Times* run frequent competitions and are worth buying regularly. In addition to their own competitions, look out also for those featured by various companies in their advertisements. Take the time to look at these advertisements; in one week's *TV Times*, I found a total of four competitions and a free prize-draw coupon.

As well as magazines, the Press has got into the competition act – and their prizes really are hitting the big time! Alongside the infamous bingo and 'scratch-off' cards, certain newspapers have recently run competitions offering luxury cars, Spanish villas, houses and even the cost of your child's private education. Before the stock-market crash in the latter part of 1987, stocks and shares were becoming a popular prize in competitions run by newspaper groups.

However, when entering such magazine or newspaper competitions, you'll need to bear in mind the readership circulations which they attract. Of course, someone has to win, but the *odds* against winning a competition in one of the popular tabloids or high-circulation women's magazines must rank alongside winning the football pools!

Ask to look at a copy of BRAD (British Rate and Data) next time you are in your local library. Inside it will give you details of all the newspapers and magazines published in Britain, together with the relevant circulation figures, then you'll see what you are up against.

While the national newspapers are much more reticent about revealing the number of competition entries they receive than their magazine counterparts, if the response to the latter is anything to go by, the *Daily Mail* should get a 5 per cent response to a competition. With a readership of 1.9 million, this means an entry of 95,000. For the tabloids with an even greater circulation that figure will, of course, be much higher.

I was somewhat surprised to learn of the competition entries received by some popular women's magazines. It would seem that those like *She*, with perhaps two competitions in addition to their Supercrozzle, do rather well in comparison with their circulation figures. *She*, with a current circulation of 212,000, tell me that they can expect, on average, a response of 22,000 for their larger, extremely challenging competitions. The Supercrozzle attracts about 3,000 entries. While *Family Circle*, with a circulation of 625,000 readers, receives between 15 and 20,000 entries for their larger double-page competitions. That is a return of only 3 per cent as against *She*'s 10 per cent. Perhaps the readers of *Family Circle* buy the magazine more for the recipes and home tips than for the competitions, even if the prize is a trip to Barbados!

Certainly enter these competitions if you regularly buy the newspaper or magazine anyway, but don't confine yourself just to them and don't be too disappointed if you have little success in winning one.

However, don't be too down-hearted. Why not look instead at other publications which attract a smaller number of readers and therefore a smaller number of potential competitors?

While looking at possible markets for my short stories, I purchased a copy of a women's magazine which features romantic fiction. In that issue was a competition for a knitting-machine and a steam-press. All I had to do was to match four knitted garments to each of four particular occasions and, believe me, the choice was fairly obvious. I won second prize, the steam-press, which was valued at £339.

If you have a hobby and buy a magazine related to your

24

interest, look out for any competitions. You might find yourself winning a piece of equipment you've always wanted but couldn't afford to buy.

For example, if you would like the chance to own a knitting-machine or a sewing-machine, one of the many magazines related to these hobbies will, at some time or another, run a competition with such prizes on offer. A fishing magazine may give you the chance of winning the new tackle you've always dreamed of. The specialist car magazines rarely offer a *car*, but what about the opportunity to acquire (for free) a variety of car accessories? It makes sense doesn't it? The readers of these magazines are interested in particular hobbies or pastimes, so they relate the prizes they offer to those subjects.

Likewise, local newspapers often run competitions with small but useful prizes, for which the entry is unlikely to even run into four figures.

The promotions department of my local newspaper told me that, on average, the number of entries they receive is about 500. Compare that to their circulation of 60,000 and you will see how low that number is. They told me there was a variation in that figure depending on the format of the competition and the prizes offered. It seems that, in my area at least, people are attracted by the chance to win lots of smaller prizes rather than just one large prize. I was told that order-of-merit and tie-breakers were avoided by the competition organisers as they tended to cause the entry figures to fall even more!

Miscellaneous
As I've said before, the sources of competitions are limitless, but to put you on the right track, here is a run-down of some more you might not have thought of.

If you visit public houses, *always* look at the drip-mats, as

25

competitions run by breweries are often to be found on these.

Never throw away leaflets which pop through your door without looking at them first. As well as useful money-off coupons, these sometimes contain little-seen competitions or prize draws. Little-seen, because most people treat them as junk mail and put them straight into the waste-bin. The big DIY stores use this method to promote their goods and offer you the chance of winning big money or vouchers to be used in their stores. Likewise inserts in magazines: why not collect them over a period of a few days and then scan them *before* consigning the competition-less ones to the dustbin?

Building societies are another source of competitions, both for adult and young savers. If you regularly save with one, look out for free magazines for savers. Competitions are particularly popular items in junior savers' magazines. If you've opened an account for your child or grandchild and they belong to a junior savers' club, make sure you point them in the right direction. Christmas could come early for them too.

Sometimes building societies will be involved in raising money for charity through promoting a competition with a fixed entry fee. The money goes to the charity (so you are spreading some goodwill) and there are usually cash prizes, invested in the building society account, for the winners.

Done any flying lately? Look in at the duty-free shops. Who knows what competitions you might find, and next time you fly it might be courtesy of one of the many companies running competitions from this source. Don't forget the in-flight magazines either.

What about your milkman? As well as promoting a wide variety of products, the leaflets left alongside your daily pinta often contain competitions. Just think of the number of people who never look at such leaflets, but drop them straight into the bin. If you save yours, it gives you a greater chance of winning.

I've just sent away for a well-known seed catalogue and by answering a few, simple questions and providing an apt slogan, I could be on my way to a luxury cruise for two. So there's another, new source for you to consider.

Remember, everywhere you shop, everything you buy and on every bit of paper that comes your way, *be on the look-out for competitions*. Believe me, there are more entry forms available each month than any individual could ever enter. Start collecting them now and the letters of congratulations could soon begin dropping through your door.

PRODUCTS AND COMPETITIONS TO AVOID

Don't waste your time looking for competitions on own-label brands – you won't find any. The reasons for this are fairly obvious. These products are sold with the minimum of fancy packaging and advertising than their big-name counterparts and represent to many shoppers the same product for less money. It's because of the need to keep overheads as low as possible that the own-label brand of product doesn't offer competitions.

I mentioned earlier that there are a few competitions which I, and many others, have come across which are not as straightforward as they seem. While in no way wishing to malign the following industries or to suggest they are hoodwinking anyone, here are my personal experiences of competitions which usually feature time-share villas and double-glazing products.

Time-share villas have become a very popular prize recently. The answers to such competitions are often ridiculously simple (for example, what is the capital of Spain?) and you might be tempted to try your hand at them. Do so by all means. If you win the first prize, it will, no doubt, genuinely be a week or a fortnight's yearly time-share, but don't be surprised if the weeks offered aren't the popular mid-summer ones. No, my advice is not so much for the winners of such competitions as to the runners-up. Often with these competitions a large number of runners-up are 'awarded' or 'selected' to receive money-off vouchers for use against the price of a holiday home. For example, I received a letter telling me that I had won half the cost of a time-share villa in Spain. (Actually I've received three such letters in the space of four months – amazing luck indeed!) The dates I could choose for my annual holiday would change the value of my voucher, but would be to a maximum of £5,000, representing half the cost of two weeks' time-share at peak holiday time. So, to take advantage of the voucher's £5,000 maximum value, I would need to *spend* £5,000 on a time-share holiday, the published price of which was said to be £10,000.

It's easy to get caught up with the excitement of receiving a congratulatory letter – I certainly did with the first one. The gorgeous pictures of fabulous properties and sunny locations featured in the glossy brochure you're also sent are there to persuade you that, above anything else, you need to own a time-share villa in Spain or Portugal or wherever. If you really did intend to buy into time-share, fine. But I've been told that such inducements to buy are used extensively in the time-share industry and are as much available to the man-in-the-street as to the lucky comper. I've made it a golden rule only to accept competition prizes if I'm not required to pay out any money of my own!

Another competition to be wary of is the one which says that success in answering the questions will be the *first step* towards winning a super prize. This is a ploy used by companies who wish to supplement their cold-calling lists, such as double-glazing firms. The idea is that by entering the competition you're deemed an interested party in the product being promoted. A salesman will then call on you and if you decide to place an order then, and only then, are you entered into a draw for the holiday or other prize on offer. Again, if you want to buy double-glazing, then the additional opportunity to win a holiday is worth looking at. But if you don't want the product, avoid these 'first-step' competitions at all cost. Remember, high-powered salesmen are very good at their jobs. If you're lured into a shop or car showroom with the chance of winning a big prize in a 'free' draw, be sure you either want to be sold something or can fend off their persuasive persistence.

BRAND LOYALTY – MAKING THE CHANGE CAN MAKE YOU A WINNER

One habit you'll need to acquire if you're going to participate in a large number of competitions is that of changing your usual brand of soap powder, washing-up liquid, beefburgers or whatever, depending on which one of the brand names is running a competition at the time. Of course, I'm not suggesting you spend more of your shopping budget than you normally do just so you can enter competitions – far from it. After all, if you regularly buy an inexpensive face cream or aftershave, you'd certainly want to think twice before buying a different brand that is twice or three times the price just because there is a competition on the pack.

No, it's those everyday products, such as washing-up liquid, that I'm talking about. Believe me, you'll find so many competitions on offer during the month you'll not need to look beyond your usual shopping list to collect plenty of entry forms!

Say, for example, that your usual brand of washing-up liquid is much the same price as one which is offering a £5,000 cash prize, isn't it worth making that change to take advantage of such a good competition opportunity?

Perhaps you normally always buy one big-name brand of frozen fish fingers and you notice that on a competitors' pack there's the chance to win a luxury holiday for two – wouldn't it make sense to buy the second brand? Who knows, you might even prefer the taste. And if not, there is nothing to stop you buying your usual brand again next time you shop.

The message is simple – whenever the cost allows you to, change your purchases to those brands which are offering competition prizes and your adaptability could soon pay off.

CHAPTER 3

HOW TO START COMPING

THE HOBBY THAT COSTS LITTLE OR NOTHING TO START

Comping is one hobby for which you'll need few 'tools of the trade'. There is no expensive paraphernalia to buy, in fact the only 'equipment' you'll need to start are a pair of eyes and an enquiring mind!

However, if you intend to enter competitions on a regular basis and, more importantly, want to maximise your chances of winning, then you'll need to organise yourself.

In the following pages I'll be outlining my own competition filing system; one that works for me and can work for you too. But please vary it to suit your own budget or ideas. Whichever way you want to follow your hobby, the important thing to remember is to set up a clear, easy-to-run system which won't let you down.

Before I start, perhaps I can make a few suggestions about the stationery I mention below. Those of you who work in an office, or know someone who does, might consider asking if there are any old, disused files lying around in the stationery office which the company might let you have for free. If not, try having a word with the stationery clerk about your requirements – perhaps she'll add them to the company order so that you get a better price than you would in the shops. After all, files can be expensive, even the simple ones I'm talking about. This

31

way you can keep costs down and maybe even manage to acquire 12 files instead of the six I'll be outlining below, with one for each month of the year.

SETTING UP A SIMPLE FILING SYSTEM
You will need:

1. A folder (or a drawer will do) in which you can keep your envelopes, writing-paper, postcards and stamps – a mixture of first and second class. There's nothing more annoying than going to the family stationery cupboard and finding someone has taken the last envelope and you have a competition closing in a couple of days! So you'll need to find a personal place in which your competition stationery is 'out-of-bounds' to anyone else. It will keep your costs down and ensure you always have the necessary requisites to hand.
2. A booklet in which to make a note of the competitions you enter, the prizes on offer (include them all – even runners-up prizes), the questions and answers you gave and your tie-breaking slogan, if applicable. The reasons for this are threefold. Firstly, it's interesting to keep a note of how many competitions you've entered over the months and what is your success rate. Secondly, organisers have an annoying habit of congratulating you on winning a prize, but often don't say in the letter what it is. Remember, you may have to wait two or three months before an announcement is made. You're likely to forget what competitions you've entered, let alone all the prizes on offer, if you don't make a note of them. Thirdly, if you do come up with a winning slogan, it's a good idea to make a note of it. By changing a few words here and there you might be able to use it, to equally good effect, in a future competition.

3. In addition to the above, I have half-a-dozen simple envelope-type files, each one labelled with the forthcoming five months (i.e. by 1 November I have a file for November, December, January, February and March competitions). The sixth file would then be labelled 'April onwards' and would contain any entry forms for competitions closing in April, May and so on. Once I've completed all my November competitions and that file is empty, I re-label it 'April'. The 'April onwards' file then becomes 'May onwards' and I transfer all my April competitions into the new April file. By circulating my files in this way as they become empty, I can keep the number I use to six. However, as I mentioned earlier, if you can afford it, or if you can get the files for free, 12 files labelled January through to December will see you through the year without the need to do this.

As I collect my entry forms, they're placed in the relevant file for the month in which the competition closes. So when I look at, say, my November file, it contains competitions closing up to 30 November, and I've three weeks in which to complete the entry forms in order to allow at least one week in which to post them before the closing date.

The reason behind my simple filing system is this. If you don't sort out your entry forms into some kind of date order, you're likely to mislay them or look at them so haphazardly that you might miss the closing date of one or two. By separating them into monthly batches, you can concentrate your efforts on the coming month's competitions while knowing that your future entry forms are safe and will not be out-of-date when you come to look at them next.

I also find it helpful to attach a sheet of paper to the outside of each file with a list of all the entry forms contained inside, with their closing dates, together with the 'qualifiers' (special wrappers, labels, etc. – see Chapter 7) needed to enter the competition. I always check this list before going shopping. There is nothing more annoying than buying Brand X and then discovering you need a Brand Y label to qualify for entry.

Some competitions 'close' on unusual dates, say for example, the 8 October. My rule is, the closer the closing date is to the beginning of the month, the better it is to play safe by putting it in the file for the preceding month. So, with the example given above, I would put an entry form closing on 8 October in my September file. It's much wiser to have a longer time to fill in your entry forms than to be rushed into sending in one with incorrect answers or a quickly thought-out slogan.

A competition which closes later in the month, say on the 20 October, would be placed in the October file, but I would asterisk it in red pen on the frontsheet of paper so I didn't forget that it needed to be sent in early.

Another advantage of the filing system is that you can ensure all the till receipts, labels or other proofs-of-purchase needed to qualify for the competition are filed together with the entry forms. By keeping everything together in a single file, there is less likelihood of one of those items getting lost.

Remember, how you work your filing system is up to you. If you're stuck for ideas, though, try mine and see how effective they are for you. Then, whenever you have a spare moment to devote to your new hobby, you can go straight to the next month's file and see at a glance what answers, slogans and qualifiers are needed, without wading through a whole pile of entry forms.

Whatever system you devise for yourself, the important rule is to safeguard against missing a competition closing date. After all, once you've passed that date with the entry form still in your possession, it's of absolutely no use to you at all. Only entries received *before* the closing date will be considered – late entries never win.

COMPING AND THE COMPUTER

Those of you lucky enough to have a home computer can keep a lot of information stored there. You'll still need the files in which to keep your competition entry forms and qualifiers, but the following are my suggestions for data file headings:

1. *Competitions for the month of . . .* This could replace the sheet of paper I mentioned above and should give you a list of competitions at a glance, with the relevant closing dates etc. But you'll need to make sure you look at this file regularly.

2. *Questions and Answers.* If you've spent a lot of time searching for the answers to a particularly challenging competition, you should consider the benefits of making a note of not just the answers, but also *where* you found them. Sometimes questions on a particular topic are duplicated over a number of competitions throughout the year – or may turn up two or three years later. Two competitions I came across in 1987 wanted to know what the letters EPCOT stood for, for example. (It's the Experimental Prototype Community of Tomorrow at the DisneyWorld Compex, Florida, USA.) You might forget the answers by simply committing them to memory. Use your reliable *computer* memory and recall them whenever you need to.

3. *Slogans.* If you've written a good slogan, store it. After all, you'll have spent some considerable time working on it. Or perhaps an idea has sprung to mind for use in a future

competition? Those without a home computer will have to write this sort of thing down on paper (and hopefully not lose it), but computer owners have the perfect way to store their good slogans and inspired thoughts. Don't risk forgetting them when the need arises – make a file for your slogans.

4. *Shopping reminders.* If you're in the habit of inputting your household requirements (perhaps you only shop once a month and keep an on-going shopping list on the computer), it's worth noting on this file the 'qualifiers' you'll need to pick up on your next shopping trip.

Don't leave your computer to gather dust or only use it to play games. Make your computer work for you. Its memory will undoubtedly prove to be much more reliable than yours in the long run!

I thought I'd found the solution to the time-consuming task of finding as many words as possible from a given phrase or slogan when, during my research for this book, I came across an advert for a computer program written specifically for compers.

I sent away for it and it conveniently arrived the day before I was due to visit my parents and brother Matthew in Lancashire; my brother, Matthew, owns a computer, I unfortunately do not. I also went armed with the details of a current word-seeking competition, the prize for which was a Mini City! Duly bribed with the promise of half the proceeds from the sale of the car if I won, Matthew began to key in the lengthy program (which ran to almost three A4 pages) and he was still at it when I returned three hours later. Eventually, with my typing, we completed it and ran it using the slogan featured in the competition rules – 'Vital for calcium'.

It was only when the screen began to fill with a selection

of jumbled-up letters that the limitations of the standard home computer became evident. A computer cannot recognise what is a 'proper' word; given such a program, all it can do is provide you with all the different permutations of letters for the word lengths specified. In this case, words of three letters or more were acceptable and so the computer began with all the different permutations it could make from the letters VITALFORCALCIUM consisting of three letters, followed by four letters and so on. I never went beyond four letters. Matthew unfortunately doesn't have a printer, so I had to sit in front of the VDU noting down not only actual words which I immediately recognised, but also those which *could* be words which I did *not* recognise.

At the end of two hours, I was almost driven to distraction and had exactly 50 known words and a whole lot more which I would have to check manually using the dictionary.

Then I looked at the example which the program-originator had sent with his written details. In order to find 66 *actual* words for a competition he had previously completed, his computer had printed out a list containing over 2,500 letter-permutations.

I decided to revert back to the dictionary. In less time than it had taken to input the program and run through only a small selection of the possible permutations for words from 3 to 15 letters long, I had found over 500 words myself. Eventually I submitted 542 words and, believe me, that was nothing compared to the monotony and boredom of watching screen after screen fill with meaningless letters!

Perhaps if you have the programming ability to run such a collection of letter-permutations against dictionary software in order to end up with actual words for a competition of this nature, you might still consider the computer a useful tool in ensuring you submit the maximum number of words possible. However, my feelings are that this way of taking part in word-search competitions isn't worth the time, trouble or expense. But then, if winning this type of competition was as simple as switching on your home computer, the organisers would soon get wind of it and we might never find another one to do again.

SHORT CUTS TO PUT YOU ON THE WINNING TRAIL

If the idea of entering competitions appeals to you but you remain unconvinced that you've the time to spend searching for forms or answers to factual questions, then you'll be relieved to hear that there are a number of publications available to help you, at a variety of costs. I've looked at three such publications, which I describe in detail below, and can only apologise to any others which have not come to my attention.

Competitors Companion

You won't find *Competitors Companion* (CC) on the newsagents' shelves as it's only available by annual subscription (currently £39.50). It's a monthly news-sheet sent to members as close to the first of the month as possible and covers a large number of competitions due to close at the end of that month. If you're interested in subscribing to CC, you can find their adverts, often full page, in a number of popular magazines (such as *Weekend* or *TV Times*) and some tabloid newspapers.

In addition to providing a solution service for its members, CC has a 'club' feel about it. Every so often the editors feature letters written by members who boast of a variety of wins and attribute this success to subscribing to CC. It also provides free advertising for readers who wish to swap or sell unwanted prizes.

The success of its members is partly guaranteed by CC who say they'll refund your subscription fee if, after one year, you haven't won at least one prize. Giving credence to my tip that regular competitors who enter more than the odd one or two competitions a month are the ones with the likeliest chances of winning, CC ask their members to enter at least five competitions per month (including the one they run for members themselves) as their side of the subscription-refund bargain.

As well as covering current and forthcoming competitions among its pages, CC gives its advice on the correct solutions to those competitions due to close at the end of that particular month. However, it's important to remember here that it's their *advice* which CC are parting with, it doesn't mean that they are always 100 per cent correct and, in fact, some questions even have them stumped from time to time.

CC's 'Winformation' pages list the prize-winning slogans for recently announced competitions which, they advise, can be used either as inspiration for your own, original slogans or which can be adapted slightly to meet a future need. In fact, I've spotted among the 'Winformation' slogans two or three which have been used to win more than one competition – virtually word for word.

Mindful of the fact that many entry forms and competition packs will have disappeared from supermarket shelves by the time the current issue appears, CC devotes two or three pages each month to listing future competitions with closing dates sometimes up to nine months in advance. In addition to detailing the first prize and the type of competition it is, CC also gives suggestions about where entry forms can be found, or the address of the promoters if entry forms can be requested by post.

Competitor's Journal and 'CJ' Special

Another publication appealing to comping enthusiasts is the *Competitor's Journal* (CJ), published fortnightly and currently costing 50p per issue. Again, it's not available at the newsagent's, but it can be ordered through them.

Like *Competitors Companion*, CJ lists, in each issue, 'Current Comps' – future competitions with the promoters' names and addresses (in case you're unable to get hold of an entry form), the closing date, details of the prizes and the type of competition it is (e.g. order-of-merit, spot-the-ball). Newspaper and magazine competitions are not covered in this list.

CJ also highlights a number of current competitions in its editorial pages, but you'll still have to find the entry forms yourself and they don't give advice on solutions. For this you'll need to subscribe to CJ Special, published monthly and currently costing £2.50 per issue. It covers those competitions received before their publication date. In the December issue, for example, it covers competitions closing from 1 December to around 15 January. These competitions are covered in full and *CJ Special* provides you with the benefit of their advice in much the same way as *Competitors Companion*.

CJ runs adverts from all sorts of individuals and companies offering, at various costs, lists of winning slogans (i.e. ones that have won competitions in the past) from which you can model your own attempts. Many of CJ's advertisers also offer an 'entry-form service' where you'll be sent a guaranteed minimum number of entry forms through the post for various monthly or annual fees. However, you'll need to bear in mind that you have no choice in which competition entry forms are sent to you and you'll still need to buy the products in order to 'qualify' for many of them. I would think that this service may be of greater value to compers with a wide variety of large stores nearby. There is no advantage in receiving Gateway or Asda's competition entry forms if you can't get to those stores for the 'qualifiers'. And if you have those stores nearby and shop at them regularly, why would you need to pay for entry forms in the first place?

CJ not only looks, but 'feels' like a tabloid newspaper, with a number of regular contributors writing on a variety of comping subjects. CJ also features its own competitions where the prizes are small, in some cases £1 to each of the first five correct entries, but it's enough to pay for two future copies of the publication.

Like *Competitors Companion*, CJ has a letters page, but these are paid for, £3 for the 'Star Letter' and £1 for each of the others. These are less of the 'I've won such and such . . .' variety, more news and views on a wide range of comping topics.

CJ's feature called 'Watchdog' is devoted to answering and upholding readers' complaints about the way in which certain competitions are run. I certainly found it an eye-opener on how heated compers can get when they feel they've been thwarted in their attempts to win a prize. However, I'm not generally sympathetic to compers who continually complain that their entry wasn't the winning one and agreed wholeheartedly with one CJ reader who wrote about how fed up she got with compers who continually dispute promoters' answers. She ended her letter with the statement that if she ever began to get upset over not winning, then she would give up. Hear, hear!

CJ obviously go to great lengths to ensure that the promoters themselves hear about any 'grouses' their readers might have and in many cases these concerns are justified. Incidentally, in one issue of CJ they shared my views about the 'awards' of time-share vouchers offered to runners-up in competitions associated with a certain time-share group (see my advice in Chapter 2).

Enter-Prize Research

This company runs adverts in *Competitor's Journal* and will send free back numbers as an example of the services it offers to potential new subscribers.

Unlike *Competitors Companion*, Enter-Prize's information is spread over a number of booklets, which can be confusing, and I'll leave it to you to decide if you can afford to subscribe to them all.

Enter-Prize's services are:

1. Their monthly *Broadsheet*, which boasts that it covers 80 to 100 current competitions each month, and provides you with their suggested solutions for each of them. It costs £4 per month, or slightly less if you subscribe half-yearly.

In addition to providing details of each competition's closing date, the prizes on offer and Enter-Prize's suggested answers to factual questions, they also include notes on *why* they have arrived at a certain order-of-merit although, as with the other publications, no one can be 100 per cent certain that their advice is correct. Another useful service is that they supply you with the answers in full. Instead of simply giving you 1/b, 2/f, 3/c, 4/d, etc. as their suggested solution, Enter-Prize would have: 1/b – Palermo is the capital of Sicily; 2/f – Majorca is the largest Balearic Island (1,465 sq. miles), etc. This is much more useful for future reference and for those competitions which will accept plain paper entries. This means that you don't need to rely on finding an entry form before you can enter and you'll be given full details of where to send your entry and by what closing date. However, as you'll read in Chapter 8, one of my prime rules for successful comping is 'Check your facts' and you'll only be able to double-check on the advice you're given in such publications as Enter-Prize's if you know what the questions are in the first place!

2. Another monthly magazine published by Enter-Prize is the *Supplement*, which costs £2 per month or £24 per year (no saving there). It contains a variety of comping information in a rather confusing format, which includes:

(a) Suggested solutions to competitions they couldn't fit into the *Broadsheet*.

(b) The actual results to previously featured competitions.

(c) Examples of winning slogans from previous competitions, together with a directory listing which past *Supplement* contains which other competition slogans.

(d) 'Reports and Retorts' – news and gossip about competitions from a wide variety of sources.

(e) Readers' letters, Pen Pals Club and free advertising section for buying or swapping prizes and entry forms.

(f) Also, listed on the back pages are competitions for which the results have been announced and winners notified.

3. *Winners' Supplement.* This is a new, quarterly publication from Enter-Prize, costing £3 per copy, which contains nothing but lists of winners' names. I wonder if so many congratulatory letters and prizes go astray to warrant bothering with a publication of this nature?

4. *Slogans.* An annual booklet, costing £2, in which tie-breaking slogans from the past year are published.

5. *Entry-form service.* Enter-Prize run two kinds of entry-form service, depending on whether you have forms to swap or not. If you have, the Forms-For-You service asks members to enclose 20 to 30 forms plus an sae and 40p, for

which they presumably receive this number of other forms in return.

If you don't have entry forms to swap, Enter-Prize's Pot-Luck-Forms are available to readers who send in 6 to 12 sae's and the charge is currently 50p per envelope.

Enter-Prize will also pay £1 to the reader who is the *first* to send in an unseen entry form. *Competitors Companion* awards a dozen 2nd class stamps and *Competitor's Journal* £1 for this service.

What neither CC nor CJ supply their members with (although there has been some discussion in both about doing so in the future) are the actual *results* of past competitions (i.e. the answers to factual questions and order-of-merits, etc.). I would have thought this would be of greatest help and interest to their readers. It's only by studying previous order-of-merit results, for example, that one can get an idea of how promoters' minds work, so you can model future order-of-merit entries on past results.

What *Competitor's Journal* in particular has considered including in its pages is the list of recent winners' names and addresses. Some companies actually advertise this information themselves in CJ's pages. I would never be interested in long lists of winning compers myself, although I get the impression that some compers are sceptical about who actually wins. In one CJ issue, the 'Watchdog' page referred to a competition won by a Mr Jones of Wales about which a number of entrants had complained – did he really exist? CJ duly reported these complaints to the company concerned's marketing manager, who was, not surprisingly, upset that anyone should think that they would try to deceive entrants by making up an imaginary winner. If that had been the case, I would have expected them to come up with someone a bit more imaginatively named than 'Mr Jones of Wales'. The problem stemmed from the fact that the winning Welshman would not agree to any publicity – not even a photograph of him receiving the keys to the car he had won! Perhaps those doubting-Thomases would be well advised to read my comments in Chapter 1.

There is no doubt that *Competitors Companion* has a large number of successful members who win big prizes month after month, so you might consider the annual fee worth paying, particularly as they guarantee one success at least if you enter the minimum suggested number of competitions they require each month. However, they don't guarantee that your prize will have either equal or greater value than your subscription. If you read this book thoroughly and want the fun of discovering competition solutions for yourself, you could find yourself being just as successful without parting with CC's membership fee.

If you don't like the idea of being a 'lone' comper, then 50p a fortnight might be a small price to pay for a chatty, easy-to-read paper like *Competitor's Journal.* It will not provide you with any solutions (for this you will need to subscribe to *CJ Special*), but having a 'Star Letter' published or winning one of its own competitions could give you a small financial return, as well as feeling that you're in touch with fellow compers.

Enter-Prize's offerings are confusingly (and expensively) spread over a number of booklets, so you'll need to be sure of exactly what information is most useful to you before subscribing. But at least you can see what you are getting *before* parting with any money if you take advantage of their free offer to potential new subscribers.

Still confused? Then take a look at my at-a-glance table which shows the costs and services offered by each of the publications mentioned above. To make this much simpler to read I've left out services like free advertising, pen-pals clubs, etc.

Publication	Annual membership fee	Solution advice?	Results of previous competitions
Competitors Companion	£39.50	yes	no
Competitor's Journal	£13.00	no	no
CJ Special	£24.00	yes	no
Enter-Prize Broadsheet	£42.00	yes	no
Enter-Prize Supplement	£24.00	yes	yes
Enter-Prize Slogans	£2.00	no	no
Enter-Prize Winners	£12.00	n/a	n/a

Published winning slogans	List of winners	Comps. where results have been announced	Notes
yes	no	yes	On average 25 A4-size pages covering solutions to 80+ competitions per issue, plus advance notice of forthcoming competitions
Some in editorial only	Some companies announce winners' names in its pages	Through editorial only	On average 24 A4-size pages in the style of a tabloid newspaper with editorial, articles and pictures of winning compers
no	no	no	Approx. 40 A5 pages of solution 'advice' covering around 100 competitions, including those found in some magazines
no	no	no	Approx. 30 A5 pages covering 80-100 comps. in full detail
yes	no	yes	Approx. 18 A5 size pages with a variety of comping information, news and views
yes	no	no	Published annually
n/a	yes	n/a	Published quarterly as long as interest warrants it

CHAPTER 4

RECOGNISING THE DIFFERENT TYPES OF COMPETITION AND HOW TO TACKLE THEM

THE 12 MOST COMMON TYPES OF COMPETITION

Basically, these are the 12 most common types of competition. How many of them have you ever seen?

- Order-of-merit
- Question and slogan
- Slogan only
- Spot-the-difference pictures
- Free draw
- Estimate
- Spot-the-ball
- Make-as-many-words-as-you-can
- Identifying the picture
- Anagrams
- Word grids
- Photographic

Of course, advertising agencies and their clients can always be relied upon to dream up all sorts of original competition ideas, as you'll read later in this chapter, but on the whole the majority of consumer competitions you're likely to come across will belong to one of these 12 categories.

Now let's look at each one in detail and I'll explain to you as fully as possible what it entails.

DETAILING WHAT'S REQUIRED FOR EACH OF THOSE 12 TYPES

Order-of-merit

This is perhaps one of the most common, but most difficult, types of competition. You'll be faced with a number of statements or points related to the product and must place them in the correct order of importance, which has already been decided upon by a team of judges. The winner will be the person who exactly, or most closely, matches that predetermined order. The greater the number of 'points' or statements to be rearranged, the greater the odds against you. For example, with six points to rearrange, the odds are 720 to 1, with seven points this rises to 5,040 to 1 and with eight, an amazing 40,320 to 1. You might think that with odds like these against you, there would be little hope of your winning except by trusting to luck. As you've probably already gathered, I don't put much faith in just luck, but I can show you how to reduce those odds by following a few, simple rules. They're ones that I follow myself and which netted me my luxury kitchen, even though the odds against me doing so should have been 40,320 to 1!

Let's suppose that you were given six points to consider when deciding upon a luxury kitchen for yourself. The competition will probably be featured on a product, such as a cereal packet, which simply acts as a 'vehicle' for the *real* prize-givers – the kitchen-design company.

Our six imaginary points are:

1. Prices to suit your pocket
2. Top-quality appliances – cooker, dishwasher, etc.
3. Excellent after-sales service
4. Professionally designed to suit your individual needs

5. Fitted by craftsmen
6. A wide range of styles to choose from

To qualify for one line, you would have to enclose one proof-of-purchase, up to a maximum of six. With odds of 720 to 1, you might consider the task wellnigh impossible. Let me show you how I would tackle this competition.

In any set of 'points' which describe a product or service, by applying some thought, you should be able to find one which you would choose as your most important factor. Similarly, one least-important point should be relatively easy to spot.

In the example I have given, point 4 would be my choice for the number one spot. Remember that the prize is a professionally *designed* and fitted kitchen. All the wonderful styles and units in the world will not compensate for bad design – a split-level oven which cuts out the light from a window, or a drawer which is almost impossible to open because of an adjacent wall, for example. So, in this example, point 4 should be your first choice for *all* the lines you're entering.

Secondly, look for the least-important point – my choice would be 3. Remember it's the kitchen company who has decided upon the correct order. They may well provide an excellent after-sales service, but that presupposes you'll encounter some problems with your new kitchen – not something they'll want to admit to. So point 3 should be your last choice for all the lines you're entering.

To improve your chances even further, is there a second important point which should feature high on your list – how about point 5? I've seen expensive units fitted by 'cowboys' and the result has been dreadful and didn't in any way reflect the excellence of the units, nor the amount of money spent on them. Likewise, a friend of mine bought units much more cheaply at a DIY store but had a professional fitter install them – the result: a kitchen which looked magnificent, at less than half the price of the bodged job. That's why 'fitted by craftsmen' would be my second choice and would follow point 4 in every line.

So now you have positioned three of the six points in a certain order, looking like this:

1. 4
2. 5
3.
4.
5.
6. 3

There are only three spaces left to fill and six possible ways in which to place the three remaining points in order. By writing down each one of these six combinations in turn, you would end up with the following six lines:

	A	B	C	D	E	F
1.	4	4	4	4	4	4
2.	5	5	5	5	5	5
3.	1	2	6	6	2	1
4.	2	1	1	2	6	6
5.	6	6	2	1	1	2
6.	3	3	3	3	3	3

The more points you can 'bank' on, the fewer attempts you will need to make, but if your three constant points are correct, and if you've thought them through carefully and logically there's no reason why they shouldn't be, the above six attempts will contain one correct solution.

When entering such order-of-merit competitions, always

start by considering *all* the information you're given – in this case, that a specialist kitchen-design company is involved. If you were to go to such a company for their advice and expertise, you would expect to pay for the two things you can't provide for yourself – professional design and expert fitting. Doesn't it therefore make sense that they'll be the two most important points in your choice? After all, if you were concerned about the price, you'd be doing-it-yourself!

A daily newspaper recently ran a series of competitions to win winter sunshine holidays. One of the points to be placed in order of priority when choosing such a holiday was: 'To soak up some winter sunshine' and in every case I made this point my first choice. The clue was *winter* holidays. Why do most people go abroad during the winter months if not to soak up the sun, when they are guaranteed only snow and cloud at home?

That brings me to another important factor when entering order-of-merit competitions – standpoint. You may hate crowds and so decide that winter holidays abroad are more enjoyable ones in July or August, but you'll need to learn to stand back from your own feelings and prejudices and judge the points on the basis of what the *majority* choose to do.

On occasion, you'll be given a specific standpoint on which to base your order-of-merit and it's important that you always bear this in mind when making your choices. One competition might ask you to make a choice from the standpoint of a young mother with two children under 5 years of age, say, or a newly married couple. If neither of these circumstances apply to you, then you'll need to take a step back and try to make your judgement from their viewpoint – not your own.

Let's take a look at the young mother with two children

under 5 and say that it's this standpoint which is required in a competition run by a store, such as Boots. There the mother can buy food, toys and clothes for her children. You have to consider the following four points and put them in order of importance to that young mother – *not* to yourself (unless, of course, you *are* a young mother with two children under 5 years of age!):

1. Friendly, helpful staff
2. Value for money
3. One-stop shopping for all your needs
4. Stores in every major high street

What would your order of importance be? My choice would be: 1/3; 2/2; 3/4; 4/1.

You've been told that the mother has two children under 5, so you can safely assume that this means pre-school children, which she will need to take with her on the majority of shopping occasions. I would consider that 'one stop shopping for all your needs' the most important point, since there's nothing worse than battling your way through door after door of shops with a push-chair and toddler in tow.

Young mothers with youngsters to feed, clothe and entertain are, in the main, likely to have little money for luxuries and will need to watch their budgets carefully. Therefore 'value for money' will be important to them.

As far as the last two points are concerned, I based my judgement on the fact that today's young mothers are genned-up with all sorts of TV adverts and magazine reports on the products they buy, therefore, apart from the girl on the till, they're less likely to be concerned about the friendliness or helpfulness of the store's staff.

If nothing else, use your common sense. Always

remember *why* people buy certain products or services. Don't be swayed by price too much. I rarely place that as my number one choice in order-of-merit competitions. If the product is a luxury item, this point wouldn't apply anyway. Sales promotion executives (those that generally dream up consumer competitions) are a vain lot and like to think that people buy their products not just because they are the cheapest on the market.

One final tip, if you're entering a number of different lines in an order-of-merit competition, please make sure no two are exactly the same!

Question and Slogan

Again, a very popular type of competition. The number of questions can vary considerably, as can the subject matter and degree of difficulty. The questions may relate to the product itself, in which case a good look at the label or packaging should produce the answers, or they may require a bit more research. In Chapter 5, I discuss the sources you could try for answering a wide variety of factual competition questions.

One tip I will emphasise here is to take a look at the questions a second time – are they really as difficult as they first appear? Sometimes, particularly with the multiple-choice type of question, only one answer is a sensible one. For example, on a recent competition entry form, one of the questions was: 'At an average speed of 10 mph, how long would it take to cycle from John o'Groats to Land's End?'

Goodness! I thought, this calls for a look at the map and some mathematics, but on further scrutiny I found that the work had already been done for me. I had to choose between two answers: (a) 87 hours 54 minutes or (b) 87 minutes. I chose, of course, (a) which just goes to show you need little more than common sense for many of the competitions around today.

I've devoted the whole of Chapter 6 to advice to guide you through writing competition slogans. I am convinced that it's these which are the stumbling-block for many people who never enter competitions, because they think that they could never come up with a good-enough slogan. Once you've read this chapter on slogan-writing, I hope I'll have changed *your* mind.

Slogan Only

Again, please refer to Chapter 6 where I cover this subject in greater depth.

Spot-the-Difference Pictures

The entry form for this type of competition usually depicts two illustrations which differ in a certain number of ways. I'm sure you'll have seen them before – this type of 'poser' is also popular in children's books and puzzle magazines. You might be asked to find 12 differences between the two pictures or, slightly harder, you might not be told how many differences there are in total.

With the former, it's just a case of checking both pictures until you have spotted the total number of differences quoted. With the latter, try imagining the pictures are divided up into six or eight squares. Taking each square in turn, check to see what differences you can find between the two. When you think you've checked the whole picture in this way, put the entry form back into your file for a day or so. Then go back and look again. It's amazing what a fresh approach turns up – differences that you missed the first time around.

Here are two more tips for entering this kind of competition. Firstly, follow exactly the directions on the entry form. If you're told to mark the differences on picture A, *do not* do so on picture B. If you're told there are 12 differences between the pictures, make sure you find and mark all 12. If you're told to mark each difference with a cross, don't circle them instead. Read the instructions *carefully* before you start.

Secondly, competitions of this nature generally have an even number of differences – most probably 8, 10 or 12. If the total number of differences is not stated and you've found 9, have a jolly good look to make sure that the 10th one hasn't escaped your notice.

Free Draw

As I've said before, this is the easiest competition you'll ever have to enter. Just write your name, address and any other information required legibly on the coupon provided and either pop it into the special box in a store or post it to the given address.

Often you needn't even make a purchase to qualify. In fact, this type of competition isn't strictly legal if a purchase is a requirement of entry, but I've seen a number of examples recently which haven't adhered to this rule. On the other hand, there are those prize draws where plain paper entries are acceptable as long as they're limited to one per envelope.

I always post free draw coupons straightaway. There are no questions to answer, no slogans to think up, so there's no point in filing them. Just make sure you have a spare envelope and stamp handy and pop it in the post as soon as you can. You'll save yourself money by using a second-class stamp as long as there's at least two weeks before the closing date.

Once again – check those rules. If there's no limit to the number of entries you can make, why not send in a few more?

Estimates

I must admit that this is not my favourite type of competition and I've yet to win anything from one. But then I never was any good at applied mathematics – you might be brilliant at this! Then again, you might know a brainy mathematician who can work out how many bars of chocolate will fit into any empty car boot, although, as you'll gather from my later comments, even this will not necessarily guarantee you a win.

Apart from the competitions which ask you to calculate how many products will fill a certain space, there are other kinds of estimating competitions, such as estimating the distance between two points. This can be either a short distance or one that takes in two points of the globe. A piece of thread, an accurate measure and a steady hand are useful tools for this job!

Or you might be shown a picture and asked to mark a particular point where 'treasure' might be found. To help you, there are generally a set of clues which you should follow. The position might be extremely obvious or you might have two or three likely spots to choose from. As with any other competition, if you have the chance to make more than one entry, *do so*.

There are also estimating competitions which involve Ordnance Survey maps. You'll be given a portion of the map to work from and a picture or description of a certain spot to be marked on the map. If map-reading is your forte, then you're certainly in with a chance.

However, I've read about people who have gone to all the trouble of driving between two parts of the country and submitting their actual mileage who *still* didn't win this kind of competition. Certainly, no competition prize would be worth the time, trouble and expense of doing this for two different countries! What the judges will be looking for is the actual figure they have in front of them, not what your answer was when you completed the task yourself. I would suggest that two separate teams filling two different car boots with bars of chocolate or whatever would arrive at two completely different answers, depending on the way they tackled that task in the first place.

So, my advice would be: look at all the information you're given and make whatever calculations you can to arrive at an *educated guess*, because that, at the end of the day, will be what will win – someone's educated guess. I only hope one day you and I will enter a winning one.

Spot-the-Ball
These are just like the versions run by the football pools promoters, but instead of a football it might be a beach ball or some other item missing from a picture. As I've said before, common sense is the best approach to this type of competition. Look carefully at the way in which the heads or hands of the people in the picture are positioned and try to imagine how they would look in real life. Draw your cross or crosses in pencil until you're sure you have made your best guess. If you can make more than one cross, then do so: the greater the number of crosses you make, the greater your chances of winning.

Make-as-many-words-as-you-can
Not a popular type of competition – either for competition setters or compers. After all, the company will have to check every one of those 657 words you have found – and you're only one of many entrants!

This is a very time-consuming competition which usually asks you to find as many words as possible from a simple slogan or phrase. I recently entered such a competition for which the prize was a time-share villa in

Spain. I was asked to make as many words as possible from 'Time-share Resorts' and with dictionary in hand, and plenty of time to spare, I found 614 – and didn't even make the runners-up! So it's up to you how many of this type of competition you enter. Luckily, they're not that common. Although the prizes are usually very good indeed, they do take an inordinate amount of time to complete. If you've time on your side and the best dictionary on the market, have a go.

By the way, those of you who own a computer might have thought, as I did, that you could get the machine to do the work for you. As you'll see from my comments in Chapter 3, that wasn't my experience. However, I'm always prepared to be contradicted and await with interest the news that an aspiring comper-cum-computer buff has solved this laborious task. Then we'll see this type of competition undoubtedly disappear altogether.

Identifying the Picture
A popular type of competition for all sorts of products. A manufacturer of car products might ask you to identify certain parts of a car, for example. Or it may be pictures of common household items taken from an unusual angle. Another variation on this theme asks you to identify famous landmarks or buildings.

In almost all cases, you'll be given a list of possible items from which to make your selection. There again, if the items are very obvious, you may be given no clues at all.

While the picture may be instantly recognisable to you, it's still always wise to check. If it isn't, Chapter 5 deals with possible sources of answers to this type of competition.

Anagrams
This is another type of competition which you either enjoy

or find completely bemusing. I never used to attempt them, convincing myself I didn't have that sort of brain – I always prefer 'easy' crosswords to cryptic clues! However, I teamed up with my mother on one occasion when we had to follow up a word-grid puzzle with a witty anagram from the letters of a product's name. We each wrote the original words on a sheet of paper and began to make as many words as we could, rather like the make-as-many-words-as-you-can competitions. The product was a popular face cream, and once I'd come up with the word 'prune' I felt we were getting somewhere. Our final anagram, 'Don't b a prune – do accost cream', won a runners-up prize of lingerie and a selection of beauty products.

Remember that with anagrams you can get away with the *sound* of letters rather than having to spell a word correctly. For example, with only two 'e's to work with, we used 'b' instead of 'be'. Likewise, you can use 't' instead of 'tea' or 'tee' and 'c' instead of 'see'.

Word Grids

With this type of competition, you're usually given a list of words which you need to circle within a grid made up of a lot of jumbled-up letters. The greater the number of words to be found, the more befuddled you may become before you've found them all. Therefore, it often helps to rewrite the original grid on a sheet of squared paper, particularly if you've been searching fruitlessly for that last word for hours. This happened with one word-grid competition that I entered a few months ago. I only had one word to find but just could *not* see where it was. Once I had sat down and redrew the grid, the missing word literally jumped out at me.

A more difficult version of this competition gives you no list of words from which to work. You're either asked to find a number of words used in the editorial or just to find as many words related to the product as possible. Again, this is a time-consuming task, but once you've got the hang of this kind of competition, it becomes easier each time. Look first for all the words related to the product which is being promoted – its name, manufacturer, the type of product it is, where it's sold, etc. When you've found these, look at the resulting letters to see if any make further words. Start at the top left-hand corner of the grid and work systematically across it, ringing any known words which come to light.

The competition instructions will give you the clues to how the words are hidden – whether diagonally, horizontally, from bottom to top, or whatever. Try and gather as many of these 'clues' and likely words before you start, crossing them off your list as well as ringing them on the grid.

Once you think you've exhausted your search, return the word grid to your file and leave it for a few days. It's surprising how a fresh mind can turn up a few more hidden words.

Photographic

An increasingly popular competition this one, particularly if photography has some direct relevance to the product being sold. You'll be told what sort of photograph to take and sometimes the rules stipulate what brand of film to use or to have your prints processed at a particular outlet.

Just to give you an idea about the variety of subjects covered by this type of competition, here are a few I've seen during the last twelve months:

- *Woman and Home* – submit a photo of your garden
- York Laboratories – photo the Volkswagen of your choice

- Tesco – photo your dog or cat in a humorous situation
- Boots Baby of the Year
- Boots Bride of the Year
- Vitbe Bread – send in a photo of yourself and family eating the product, to fit into a category of adventure, family or humour
- Picture yourself with a diet cola
- Boots Mum in a Million – photograph your Mum

As with any other competition, it's important to read the rules precisely. If the organisers want something 'witty', keep your subject matter amusing. If you're asked to include a product, for example a brand of fizzy drink, make sure that it's prominent.

One competition I entered asked for a picture of whichever model of car entrants wanted to win, within a certain manufacturers' range. I spent days searching for my chosen car, trying to make it as prominent as possible. However, I was working very much in the dark on this one and didn't win. No competitor can be certain exactly what will appeal to a particular judge in the photography competition, but if you're an avid photographer and enjoy taking creative pictures, you may have better luck than I have had so far.

THE SKY'S THE LIMIT – OTHER COMPETITIONS TO WATCH OUT FOR

The list I gave you earlier was of the 12 *most common* types of competition. That doesn't mean they're the only formats which competition organisers stick to – far from it. There could be no end to the variety of competitions on offer in the future, and who knows what will be popular in 10, 15, or even 20 years' time, when no doubt we'll have dispensed with entry forms and be entering competitions on the ubiquitous home computer instead. Maybe some of the competitions I'll mention here will become more popular in the years to come.

Send in a recipe using the product

A cunning way by competition organisers of ensuring that entrants are users of the product! If you genuinely use the product regularly and have a favourite recipe, you could be on to a winner here as I wouldn't have thought this a particularly popular competition. You'll need, however, to check the rules about whether you can use a recipe you've found in a book, or whether it has to be one you have put together yourself – the latter is the most common as judges are looking, as with all other competition types, for original ideas.

Tips

Manufacturers of beauty or health products sometimes feature competitions where entrants are asked to send in their favourite tips – be it how to look after your skin or hair, or a tip for healthy living. The most popular prize for winners of this type of competition is a stay at a health farm. Having spent a long weekend at one myself, I can assure you it's a prize worth winning!

Again, originality is the key here and it's no use just copying something out of a book. If you make up your own body lotion, have an age-old recipe for improving skin blemishes or follow a special regime for an ailment-free life, then write it down – your tip might just win.

Crosswords

I haven't seen too many of these around, although some magazines, like *Family Circle*, feature a regular 'Prizeword'.

With crossword competitions, the clues are usually written with the product in mind and the answers found by reading the labels or packaging. This type of competition is unlikely to be much more challenging than that, but if you do come across a difficult one, say in an upmarket magazine or newspaper, a useful book to have by your side is *Chambers' Crossword Manual* (Chambers), in which the author – who compiles crosswords himself – details the different types of crossword and provides tips on how to deal with each one. There are also 80 crosswords with which to sharpen your wits!

If there is a tie-breaker for this type of competition, you'll usually be asked to provide an alternative for one or two of the given clues.

Match Noises to Objects

Duckham's Oil recently ran a 'Match the Engine Noise to the Car' competition, the prize for which was a magnificent Ford Sierra Cosworth worth £16,000, but my goodness it wasn't easy. The competition featured a telephone number for several regional locations from which callers would hear the engine noises of several different cars (the names of which were provided). Entrants had to match the noise of each car engine to the relevant car name.

Perhaps car enthusiasts are more atuned to the sound of engines than I am – I could only identify one with any certainty, and that was the London taxi! A competition for experts or very lucky guesses, I think.

Balloon Races

Another unusual competition in which successful entrants have a balloon marked with their name and address. At an appointed time and place, these are all released and the one which reaches the furthest distance and is returned to the competition address is deemed the winner.

It really is down to luck whether you win with this type of competition. Even if your balloon does reach a far-off destination, there's no guarantee that it will be found, or even that the finder will return it.

Scratchcards

A similar idea to the cards issued frequently by the popular Press. I've seen a number of different examples of them recently. One was a novel alternative to 'spot the ball', where a number of different spots were available and the comper had to scratch off only one to see if the ball or blank space was underneath.

Similarly, a roulette wheel has been featured in one competition, with the comper asked to scratch off one square only to win £10 if the roulette ball is found – pure luck. Another version asked compers to scratch off one multiple-choice to a number of questions.

In all these cases, only one 'scratch' was allowed – any more and the entry was disqualified. To enter this kind of competition the comper should ignore the 'scratchcard' idea and look at it as a straightforward 'spot the ball', multiple-choice or question competition instead. The one advantage with this type of competition, of course, is that you get the results straightaway.

Phone-Ins

An increasingly popular type of competition and one, I think, which will cause consternation among compers once they receive their phone bills and see the hidden costs involved.

Phone-in competitions are rarely free, using as they do numbers which are charged at several times the standard rate of a phone call. Some tapes start at the beginning for each call received, some run continuously and the caller will need to wait until the tape begins again before making any sense of the competition. Either way, your call will last at least three minutes and the cost, which may or may not be specified on the entry details, could be as high as 38p *per minute* (the current peak-time rate at time of writing).

It's up to you how many, if any, of these competitions you choose to enter, but if your phone bill is unusually high next quarter, don't say I didn't warn you!

Colouring Competitions

My list wouldn't be complete without mention of one competition specifically directed at children – the one where they're asked to colour in a picture.

I often wonder how judges can choose between the efforts of, say, a 4-year-old and a 7-year-old, particularly when the age ranges in each category are so wide. Suffice it to say that this is a very subjective competition, where 'beauty' is very much in the eye of the beholder. However, it's also one which can give your children an enjoyable half-hour in addition to possibly winning them a prize.

I don't see anything wrong in encouraging children to enter competitions. My son Graeme has enjoyed entering them ever since I became interested myself, and he's only 5 years old. Luckily, children, the younger ones particularly, have very short memories and are unlikely to remember two months' hence that they haven't yet received a letter of congratulations. My own son has also learned a very useful rule – that winning isn't automatic: you have to work for it. But if you make your best attempt, your chances of winning are as good as anyone else's.

CHAPTER 5

WHERE TO FIND YOUR ANSWERS

SOURCES FOR ANSWERING COMPETITION QUESTIONS

When you become an avid comper, you'll find yourself spending a lot of time in the reference section of your local library. There you'll find a whole range of books from encyclopaedias to specialised works on opera, poetry, art and the like, from which you can usually find the answers to most questions set in competitions. A few hours can be quite profitably spent searching out the answers required to complete your entry forms and it can be a satisfying, relaxing way to broaden your knowledge at the same time! Then again, I've spent a whole morning looking for the answer to one remaining question, returning home dejected because it had eluded me. That's the challenge (and for me the enjoyment) of entering competitions. It's rather like being an amateur sleuth trying to seek out clues and solve a mystery.

Of course, once you know where to look for answers, that's half the battle. The trouble is, some questions are so phrased that, unless you know the answer straight out, you have absolutely no idea where to start. I remember that, in order to complete the *Listener*'s 'Mastermind' competition (for a holiday for two in India) I needed only eight elusive answers to a total of 100 questions. One of these was 'Where would you be if you could see the Merry Men of

May in play?' I immediately thought of morris dancers and the maypole, and read page after page about these subjects, but without finding what I was looking for. My father suggested it might have something to do with astronomy; and one bright spark suggested I work my way through the complete works of Shakespeare, as they were surely one of his characters! I looked for hours at a wide variety of subjects only to find that there was no reference to 'Merry Men of May'. Becoming more and more despondent, I sat one morning in my local library when, purely by chance, I began to flick through the pages of *Brewer's Dictionary of Phrase and Fable*. Suddenly, there was my answer – a stretch of bubbling water in the Stroma Channel, Pentland Firth!

Even great detectives need to rely on strokes of luck as well as strokes of genius, so don't give up – keep searching, no matter how elusive you think an answer might be. After all, the competition organisers must have got the information from somewhere. Think of the plus side to all this extra reading and how much additional knowledge you're accumulating in the process.

As far as libraries are concerned, it always pays to make friends with your local librarian. They're generally very well-read and can at least point you in the right direction if not give you the answer you need outright. Don't be shy about the reasons why you want the information. Comping is a fascinating subject, as much to those who don't take up the hobby as to those who do. You might even end up converting your librarian to trying a few competitions!

Don't forget that national newspapers keep a valuable store of information in their own libraries – particularly with reference to those long-forgotten national events. While I'm not suggesting you ring them regularly (Whitaker's *Almanack*, the *Daily Mail Year Book* or *Pears*

Cyclopaedia will supply the majority of current affairs information you'll need), a once-in-a-while query wouldn't do any harm. I needed to know the racing colours of the Queen and Queen Mother and rang the sports section of my favourite national newspaper. The journalist who answered my call was very helpful and saved me hours of reading books on horse-racing in order to extract this information.

On another occasion, one question I had to tackle in a competition asked, 'For what feat was a prize offered in 1909 by the London *Daily Mail*?' There was no clue to what this noteworthy act might have been. Where did I start? By ringing the library of the *Daily Mail*, that's where. The man who spoke to me was reluctant to pore over all 365 copies of the newspaper for 1909 but, after a quick chat with his colleagues, the suggestion that it might have something to do with Blériot's first Channel crossing by plane put me on the right track. I looked up a reference to Louis Blériot in the *Encyclopaedia Britannica* and was delighted to find that he did indeed receive a prize from Lord Northcliffe, owner of the *Daily Mail*, in 1909.

Similarly, don't forget to make enquiries with your local newspaper for any questions you might get relating to local events.

I had all but one answer to a very interesting and challenging competition whose questions were all about India. (As you've probably gathered by now, I'm trying my hardest to win a holiday to that wonderful country!) The question was 'Is *Misti Doi* an Indian dish or not?' It certainly sounded Indian, I reasoned, but had it been put in as a red herring (if you'll excuse the pun!)? I love Indian food and have a number of cookery books on the subject at home, but I could find no reference whatsoever to *Misti Doi*. I was complaining about this lack of success to my friend, Anne, when she suggested I telephone the Indian Embassy. There was my most obvious source of information and yet it had never occurred to me. The lady at the Embassy couldn't have been more friendly or helpful and was delighted I was taking such an interest in her country's cuisine. Yes, she told me, *Misti Doi* is an Indian dessert. I was then able to send off my answers, satisfied that they were all correct. Unfortunately, I didn't win the trip to India which I wanted, but felt a great sense of achievement in having completed all those difficult questions correctly.

Then again, you don't need to go to such lengths straightaway. I'm sure you have friends or family who have a particular knowledge of, say, sporting facts or current events. In fact, please don't think that all competition questions are as difficult as the ones I've mentioned above – they're not. But the point I want to make is this: just because a certain answer eludes you, don't assume that no one else knows the answer. You'll kick yourself if, after searching fruitlessly for an answer for hours, a member of your family informs you that they knew it all along – if only you'd asked!

THE BEST SOURCES OF INFORMATION FOR THE 12 TYPES OF COMPETITION

Let's now look at how particular sources of information can help you with some of the competition formats.

Order-of-Merit

The best way to understand the important points relating to a particular product is to look at the product literature, if possible. If not, examine the labelling or any information given on the pack. Are there any points about the product which are emphasised over and over again or given prominence in the advertising material? If you know the important points being stressed by the manufacturer about the product, you're that much nearer to knowing how to complete the order-of-merit.

One very valuable source of information is the results of past order-of-merit competitions. Get into the habit of sending an sae with your entries and study the results when you receive them. How close was your entry to the actual result? Where did your choices vary, and why? Only by examining what judges have chosen in the past will you have a better chance of getting your order-of-merit entries correct in the future.

As I've said before, this is a difficult competition to tackle with 100 per cent certainty, but if you read my tips in Chapter 4 and put them into practice, you should be giving yourself a better-than-average chance with competitions of this kind. If all else fails – use your common sense.

Question and Answer

I don't have any problem nowadays answering the question 'What would you like for your birthday/Christmas?' The answer is always 'a reference book' and I then go on to tell the enquirer which one I would like. One day I might be lucky enough to find a rich relative who will buy me a set of *Encyclopaedia Britannica*!

There are vast numbers of extremely useful reference books to be found in bookshops, or in your local reference library if you don't want to buy too many. If, however, you do want to increase the number of books you own yourself, my advice would be to keep them as general as possible. I've been taking part in a 'Rum Challenge' recently where the questions are all about rum and how it's made. But I wouldn't dream of buying a book on the subject. It's not likely to be much use to me in the coming months unless all the rum companies decide to hold competitions. So if you're going to buy reference books, keep the subject range as wide as possible and use the more specialised works in the library to browse through on one of your 'investigative mornings'.

For details about the publications which I find of greatest help when answering general-knowledge questions and for suggestions as to what to buy when setting up your own home library, please read the last section of this chapter.

Estimates

For travel estimates, you'll need an up-to-date atlas of the world and perhaps the odd travel brochure. If you're asked to find the minimum distance between two places in the world by a variety of different travel methods, why not pop into your local travel agent and pose them the question? For all they know, you could be a potential traveller concerned at covering too many miles in too short a space of time!

When estimating the number of boxes or packets that will fit into a car boot, for example, get the relevant brochure from your nearest car showroom. These contain a wealth of information and specifications, one of which will be the cubic capacity of the boot. If you have a mathematical genius in the family or perhaps someone you know is taking A-level maths or is at university, why not give them this type of teaser to solve for you?

Spot-the-Ball

If the picture you're asked to mark is an actual event from sporting history, why not have a look through some books on the subject to see if the match or game you're looking for is pictured there? A long shot, admittedly, but how do the competition organisers know the correct placing of the ball? Unless you know how a game is played and the different 'shots' involved, you're less likely to place your cross in the right area. The rest is pure chance, but if the picture is a big one, you'll improve your chances if you know roughly where the ball *should* be.

Make-as-Many-Words-as-You-Can
An up-to-date dictionary is essential for this type of competition – often the rules state which one it should be. (Please also see my comments about a computer in Chapter 3.) There's no easy short cut to this time-consuming competition. However, a lot of people are put off entering competitions of this type because of this, so your entry will stand a greater chance if you're methodical and thorough.

You should begin by reducing the letters in the given phrase or slogan so no two letters are the same. Are there any 'major' letters missing – e's, s's, or n's for example? Train your eyes to skip over any words which contain these, but make sure you include every possible spelling of the word you're including – both 'favour' and 'favor' are listed in the *Concise Oxford Dictionary* as being acceptable. Don't forget to look at the back of the dictionary, either, as there is often an addendum of new words which have been recently introduced into the language.

Identifying the Picture
Don't forget the general section of your library when looking for the solution to this kind of competition. There you'll find books on car maintenance which can identify car parts, and ones on history or tourism which could be helpful in identifying a building or particular landmark.

If you know someone who works in engineering or the

technical trades, that completely baffling picture might make sense to them straightaway. Don't be frightened to ask. After all, if you choose your moment and make sure that the person you want to ask is not rushed off his or her feet, they're unlikely to refuse your request just for the sake of it.

Anagrams and Word Grids
Again, you'll find that the best dictionary you can buy will be the most invaluable tool for solving these 'teasers', although there is a book entitled *Longman's Anagram Dictionary* by R. J. Edwards (published by Longman) which is simple to use and lists over 200,000 common anagrams from 3 to 15 letters long.

Photograph
As I've said earlier, it's difficult to know exactly what the judges are looking for with this type of competition, but if you're given a particular subject to photograph (say, a happy moment or someone enjoying the product being promoted), then it would be a good idea to have a look at some 'coffee table' books on photography and take your inspiration from the pictures you find there. Like any other competition, the judges will be looking for something different, or the subject tackled in an unusual way. By looking at how the top photographers have 'shot' their subjects, you might hit upon exactly the right idea.

BUILDING UP YOUR HOME LIBRARY
I love books – especially reference books. They're a never-failing source of fascinating facts on an ever-widening variety of subjects and indispensable to the aspiring comper. The greater the number of books you have on your

own book-shelves, the more time you'll save in entering factual competitions as you'll need to spend less time in your local library.

For obvious reasons, I cannot include every book which would help with every type of competition you're likely to come across – that would take a much larger amount of space than I have here. What I can do, however, is to give you a list of those books I've purchased myself, to tell you what they contain and how they've helped me with past competitions. I've included the names of the authors and publishers but not prices, as these might be out of date anyway by the time you read this book. Also, you might be able to buy cheaper versions from book clubs or during sales.

Of course, factual answers aren't the only reason to buy many of the reference works I'll tell you about: they can be of the greatest help when writing those tie-breaking slogans, so I've divided my list into two sections – books for facts and books for slogans.

How much money you can afford to spend will, of course, dictate how many, if any, of these books you choose to buy yourself (or better still, have bought for you as birthday or Christmas presents). But the beauty of the ones I've listed is that they provide helpful and interesting information for a variety of other uses, as well as being invaluable aids to the serious comper.

Books for Facts

1. *A set of Encyclopaedias.* Of the various ones available, I prefer *Britannica* or *Colliers*. If you're lucky enough to own a set of encyclopaedias already, then you won't need me to tell you how valuable they are. However, they're expensive to consider purely on the basis of entering competitions.

One alternative to buying a completely new set is to ask your local library whether they sell out-of-date sets cheaply to the public. You can often pick these up for £50 or so. You'll need to bear in mind that older volumes of encyclopaedias won't have up-to-date information on populations, recent scientific discoveries, new technology and the like. Even geographical boundaries and country names change over the years. But for historic facts and other unalterable data, a second-hand set of encyclopaedias will be a good basis on which to build your home library.

If, like me, you can't afford a whole set of encyclopaedias and are unable to pick them up second hand, a single encyclopaedic volume could be the answer. The *Macmillan Encyclopaedia*, which I bought recently, has 25,000 entries from Aachen (a spa city in West Germany) to zygote, and 1,234 illustrations. The inside cover shows the star configurations of the Northern and Southern Hemispheres. There's a family tree of Kings and Queens of England from William I to the House of Windsor, with dates of reigns. There are colour plates, including ones on the human body, maps of the world, flags of the world – all in a total of 1,376 pages. While none of the subjects is covered in the detail to be found in a complete set of encyclo-paedias, the facts given are usually pertinent enough to answer all but the most demanding competition questions.

2. *The Reader's Digest Book of Facts* (Reader's Digest). Any book by the Reader's Digest is worth owning. This one has provided me with the answers to many competitions in the past. In over 400 pages, it covers a whole range of facts about people and places, science and technology, animals and plants, arts and entertainment, the earth and the universe, easily accessed by the

comprehensive index at the end. Even when not helping you with competition questions, this book will provide you with hours of reading entertainment.

3. *The Guinness Book of Records* (Guinness Books). This is a regular on my Christmas list, particularly as its usefulness depends very much on it being bang up-to-date. Never rely on an old copy, as the records described within may have been superseded. Obviously, facts about people or things which are 'firsts' in certain fields will not change – they're historic facts – but sporting and other human achievements are liable to alter from one year to the next. Its 300+ pages are packed with such a variety of facts and information, that this book will always be of vital importance to the serious comper.

4. *The Shell Book of Firsts* by Patrick Robertson (Treasure Press, 1983 edition). In his introduction, the author explains that this 264-page book is a collection of 'firsts' which have changed society and in some way contributed to the life we live today. As such, therefore, it's not a complete list of every 'first' to have happened.

The extensive index lists those subjects which are covered in depth, in the alphabetical listings. Those subjects not detailed in this way are dated and can be referred to in the chronology of dates running from AD 767 to 1983 (the latest edition). If you need to know when the first telecast of a sporting event took place (17 February 1931), or the name of the man who first introduced the permanent wave (Karl Ludwig Nessler), then this book will provide the answers.

5. *The Concise Oxford Dictionary of Quotations* (Oxford University Press). There are many such volumes on the market, but I like this handy, paperback version because it's an inexpensive, yet comprehensive, compilation of the most notable quotations in literature – nearly 6,000 of them.

6. _The Concise Oxford Dictionary_ (Oxford University Press). No home should be without a good dictionary. Its use is vital for checking the spelling or meaning of even the most commonly used words in the English language. How many people do you know, for example, who frequently misspell or misunderstand the correct use of the words 'principle' and 'principal', or who say they want to lend something from you when they really mean borrow? Obviously they don't own or refer to a dictionary.

This volume has saved me many an extensive search with its 40,000 main entries and 74,000 other vocabulary items.

I use it not only to find the answer to factual questions, such as what is a lahar (a flow of volcanic mud), and to check on any obscure wording in competition rules, but also when I need to know the monetary units for any country in the world, weights and measures (imperial and metric), how to convert Fahrenheit to centigrade or vice versa, the meaning of abbreviations and initials, chemical symbols, or the etymology of words taken from another country and introduced into the English language, such as tandoori (from the Indian, _tandoor_, meaning a clay oven).

These are only the uses to which I put my dictionary when answering factual questions. It also has its uses when I'm looking for inspiration with slogans, but I'll deal with that later.

Even if you buy no other reference book for your home library, then I hope I've persuaded you that an up-to-date dictionary is essential to the comper.

7. _The Times Concise Atlas of the World_ (Times Books Ltd). Not only an indispensable reference work for countries and places in the world, with almost 150 full-colour maps, you'll also find within its pages the following facts:

(a) The status (i.e. whether a principality, republic, etc.) capital, area, population, language and currency of over 180 countries;

(b) The estimated population figures for the largest metropolitan areas in the world;

(c) Lake areas;

(d) River lengths;

(e) Mountain heights;

(f) Areas and greatest depths of the world's oceans and seas;

(g) Pages on how the world was formed, natural phenomena, atmosphere and climate, water resources and vegetation, mineral deposits and their uses, food and nutrition, population variations, fuel and energy, the universe, areas of the moon and much, much more.

8. *A Great Britain Road Atlas.* Essential for calculating the distance between two points in Britain. The larger towns and cities are usually already tabulated for you.

9. *The Guinness Book of British Hit Singles* by Paul Gambaccini, Tim and Jo Rice (Guinness Books). Covering every single hit since 1952, this is *the* book for answering questions on pop music from Pearl Carr and Teddy Johnson to The Cars, from Bert Weedon (remember him?) to WHAM!

You'll find here the date when a certain record first hit the charts, the correct title, label and catalogue number, the highest position reached and the number of weeks it stayed in the charts – all in alphabetical order by artist or group.

If you know the name of the single but not the artist or group who sang it, you can look this up in the comprehensive index at the back, which lists them alphabetically by title.

There really is a whole wealth of information between its covers, detailing popular music from the inspired to the inferior!

10. *Brewer's Dictionary of Phrase and Fable* (Cassell Ltd). This book has only helped me with one competition question so far (the Merry Men of May, referred to on page 67), but it's so fascinating that I love to delve into it just for the sake of it, and I'm sure it will prove to be a worthwhile purchase for years to come.

In over 1,200 pages, it details the derivation, source and meaning of phrases, figures of speech, names and words, both old and contemporary, which have a story attached to them. Thus we find that 'abacus' was the name given to the different counting devices first used by ancient civilisations of the Mediterranean and China. The word itself comes from the Greek *abax*, meaning a tablet covered in dust or sand.

This is a wonderful book for anyone fascinated by words or phrases and their meanings. For the more obscure, factual questions, it will undoubtedly prove useful.

11. *The Book of Ingredients* by Philip Dowell and Adrian Bailey (Michael Joseph). A comprehensive, pictorial display of foodstuffs and drinks, with details of where they originate and how they're used. With this book to hand, you'll never again mistake your ceps from your chanterelles! (These are two different types of woodland mushroom, in case you didn't know.)

12. *The RSPB Book of British Birds* by Peter Holden and J.T.R. Sharrock (Macmillan). Coloured illustrations and fully informative text on the habitat and habits of the birdlife which graces Britain's coasts, countryside and towns.

13. *The Good Housekeeping Cookery Book* (Guild Publishing). A good, standard cookery book with interesting

information on cuts of meat, fish, cheeses, wines and liqueurs, as well as the ingredients and method of preparation for a vast range of everyday and luxury dishes.

14. *Kings and Queens of England and Scotland* by Allen Andrews (Marshall Cavendish). Over 1,000 years of British monarchy from Egbert (802–839) to Queen Elizabeth II, with information on each individual's date of birth, succession, marriage, children and death, together with a short biography of their life and times.

15. *The Reader's Encyclopaedia* (Harper & Row, 3rd edition). Over 9,000 entries covering every aspect of literature – classic and contemporary, biographies of writers and their historical subjects, plot sketches and those of some principal characters from the world of books. In fact, everything you would need to know to answer questions on literary references. Not only useful to the comper but a fascinating work besides.

Books for Slogans

1. *Nuttall's Dictionary of Synonyms and Antonyms* (Guild Publishing). I'm forever leafing through this valuable work when thinking of slogans. It enables me to find words of similar meaning (synonyms) or ones of opposite meaning (antonyms) to the ones I have in mind. For example, when confronted with the opening words of a slogan such as 'Directional Sanilav points to household hygiene because . . .', I find the relevant 'thematic' words – in this case 'directional' and 'points' and find a variety of other words of similar meanings to help me complete that sentence in an apt way.

2. *Roget's Thesaurus* (various publishers). A well-known book but one I doubt many people use. A thesaurus is not a collection of synonyms, more a source of words which

express the same idea or closely-related ideas. Therefore, a slogan with a theme of 'holiday' can be linked with words associated with absence, leisure, ease and recreation. The large number of words to be found under each of these four headings is bound to give you some inspiration for word play or common phrases which can all be used in the context of 'holiday'.

Once you're acquainted with how a thesaurus works you'll see how ideal it is for the thought-provoking comper.

3. *Whitfield's University Rhyming Dictionary* by Jane Shaw Whitfield (Barnes & Noble). An invaluable aid to rhyming words which are less common, this handy paperback concentrates on the five vowel sounds and the variations derived from them. It's easy to use and, of further value to the comper, includes colloquial and slang expressions not found in many works of this type.

One of the best ways of writing a winning slogan is by steering clear of the usual, often-used rhymes which are bound to be re-hashed by compers, whether intentionally or unintentionally. By using the rhyming dictionary, the comper can choose a rarer description of the competition product or company and almost always find a suitable word with which it will rhyme.

4. *The Newnes Crossword Dictionary* (Newnes Books). An invaluable aid for the crossword addict, this book also has its uses for the comper. Approximately 130,000 words are classified in main subject categories, such as 'domestic', 'famous people', and 'geography', from which subdivisions, such as 'drinks', 'explorers' and 'islands', plus many, many more, are indexed. Under each subdivision, the words are split into those containing four, five, six or more letters, all set out alphabetically. Its comprehensive lists of animals, coins and currency,

composers, biblical characters or nautical terms make it an extremely useful book for the comper looking for inspiration.

A music competition, for example, might ask you why you relax by your record-player. Under the list of composers, you'll find a comprehensive collection of names, from which you might choose: 'It's such *Bliss* after a *Bizet* day'; or 'It helps me nod *Orff*'; 'It's my *Lully*-by – I can un-*Ravel* my thoughts'; 'I can relax after a *Bizet* day's *Chopin* (shopping)'.

You see, the clues are all there. You just need to put them all together.

5. *The Dictionary of Puns* by John S. Crosbie (Futura). I love this little paperback – I always get a good giggle from it, and it has provided me with some witty, if contrived, ideas for humorous slogans.

6. *The Concise Oxford Dictionary* (Oxford University Press). Not only can you check upon the actual meaning of a word found from another source, but the dictionary also includes, in the relevant entry, the various common phrases or sayings associated with that word.

A toilet-cleaning product might, for example, be marketed on the effectiveness of its cleaning 'power'. From the clue-word 'power', you'll find listed in the dictionary: 'more power to you', 'more power to your elbow', 'the powers that be', 'power pack', 'power house' and 'power point' – any one of which could be used effectively in a slogan endorsing that product.

CHAPTER 6

SLOGANS – WAXING LYRICAL ABOUT THE PRODUCT

HOW YOU CAN WRITE WINNING SLOGANS

I've found this, of all the chapters in this book, the most difficult one to write. Not because of any lack of material – on the contrary, there's so much to write on the subject of slogans that it was difficult to know where to start.

If I had £1 for every time I've heard the excuse, 'I never enter competitions because I can't write slogans', I'd be a rich woman by now. I believe it's the single biggest factor which prevents the majority of people from entering competitions on a regular basis. They see the words 'complete the following sentence in no more than ten words', and normal, intelligent and lucid people just fall apart!

Slogan-writing can be mastered, like riding a bike or knitting a jumper, and once you've learned a few, simple techniques, you'll wonder why you ever worried about it in the first place. I'm not saying I can teach you how to win every competition which asks for a slogan tie-breaker: I certainly don't; and it would be foolish of me to say you will, too. After all, judging, whether it be a baby contest or the local horticultural show, is a very subjective exercise. The ugliest baby you've ever seen might win that bonny baby competition; a joke that has everyone falling about might leave you flat. So it is with competitions. You might consider your amusing one-liner to be brilliant, but the judges dismiss it without a second look – who knows what appeals to different people? But if I can show you how to start, where to find inspiration and what the judges are looking for, you are more than half-way towards writing winning slogans yourself.

Competitions are won and lost on two great 'unknowns': the standard of entries received and the personal preference of the judging panel. That's what makes comping such a challenge. Strange though it may be to admit, I wouldn't want to win every competition I entered. If I knew I was definitely going to win, it would take the 'spice' out of this absorbing pastime. I prefer the challenge of pitting my wits and talents against an unknown number of compers and judges I've never met.

These 'unknowns' can also work to your advantage. Unless it has been written into the rules that prizes are awarded only to entries of a certain standard, compers will win runners-up prizes because either there hasn't been a large enough entry, or because the standard was so low that even the most banal of slogans won – causing those of us who write for the result to exclaim, 'How on earth did someone win with *that*!' One PR executive I spoke to on the subject told me that good slogans are few and far between. That must mean that those compers who spend a bit of time and take a little trouble to think about what's required, could 'sweep the board' on a number of occasions when the overall standard of slogans is poor.

Panellists change from competition to competition, even when two competitions are run by the same company in one year, so it's wellnigh impossible to say with any certainty that a specific slogan will appeal in one case or another. However, by studying past winning slogans, you'll be able to see what has previously caught the judges' eye. If you subscribe to *Competitors Companion*, for example, you'll have the opportunity to see what type of slogan has appealed in the past to Tesco's judges, say, or to the manufacturer of a particular product, because CC devotes two or three pages per issue to winning slogans. Some judges *love* verse (I'll go into this in greater detail later); some prefer clever plays with words; others like flattering comments about their products. But there's one common denominator – they're all looking for something a bit *different*: 'with a bit of a lilt to it' were the words used by one man I spoke to about competition judging.

Before I talk about the 'nuts and bolts' of slogan-writing or give you exercises to try for yourself, here are some points to bear in mind so that, to the best of your ability, you're giving the judges exactly what they want to see.

Originality

Don't think you can regurgitate the company's own advertising slogan and walk away with a major prize. The majority of competitions ask for *original* sentence completions, so the judges will not expect to see their own slogans repeated in verse, although advertising material or slogans you've seen before can be used to good effect in a completely different context and with your own, original embellishments. It will help you to know what the company says about its product, but you should adapt these positive points in your own original way.

All the comping publications, and certain adverts within them, love to emphasise how previous winning slogans can help compers to write prize-winning ones themselves. The idea is that by changing a few words here or there – Presto for Gateway, baked beans for fish fingers, for example – you can come up with a second, almost identical, but equally successful slogan. There's no doubt that this has worked for some compers in the past and they've done very nicely from such blatant plagiarism. However, there are such things as 'old chestnuts' – slogans which have been around almost since the dawn of time, resurrected by hopeful compers who expect to drive off with a car or sail away on a cruise simply by dusting them down once more. The risk in doing the same is that sitting on the judging panel might be one of the 'comping fraternity' who has seen such revitalised 'old chestnuts' a thousand times before and will throw them out of the running without a second look. While pages of winning slogans can make interesting and entertaining reading, how will you know which are the most infamous 'old chestnuts' if you arbitrarily pluck one out of the lists and use it yourself? Far better to start off with an original idea of your own and adapt that – as often as you like. After all, it was your brainchild – wasn't it?

Aptness

The beauty of having to complete the *end* of a sentence is that you're often given some clues about what the judges will be looking for. In other words, the opening words should suggest a theme to you (although there are many, many compers who never see this and go off on a tangent of their own) and the winning slogan will be the one which maximises the use of such a theme.

Let's play a little game. I'll write down five opening sentences. Each should suggest to you a clue about how the sentence should be completed. Write down only those words which provide you with the 'key' to that theme, to be continued throughout the completed sentence, and see whether you are 'clued' up to writing successful slogans.

1. Two's company with Colgate at Tesco because . . .
2. Ordnance Survey maps are the best way to find Britain's hidden treasures because . . .

3. My sound advice is always to shop at Boots because . . .
4. Shopping at Superdrug is electrifying because . . .
5. I give Jacob's and Hovis Cream Crackers more than a sporting chance because . . .

Seeing the relevant entry forms would have made this exercise even simpler because all the prizes offered for these five competitions also hinted at the 'theme'. The prizes were:

1. Gleneagles weekend and a car (double prize)
2. Gold sovereigns
3. Compact disc player
4. Electricity bill paid for a year (£1,000 max)
5. Tickets to a sporting event

Are you any nearer to solving the 'clues'? Did you write down:

1. Two's company (i.e. 'partnerships')
2. Hidden treasures (i.e. gems, wealth, gold)
3. *Sound* advice (i.e. music)
4. Electrifying (i.e. electricity)
5. Sporting chance (i.e. sports, games)

Well done if you spotted them all. If you didn't, I hope this exercise went some way to showing you what to look for in the future.

Now all you have to do is decide what to write, but at least you have your 'theme' to start with. Why not have a look at your thesaurus and see what words or ideas you can come up with for each of these five themes?

88

Here are some to help you:

1. Two's company. Think of any famous partnerships, but make sure they're not too obscure or from the dim and distant past or the judges might not get the connection.

When I entered this competition, which, incidentally, involved matching five famous people with their equally famous partners, I thought of Sherlock Holmes and Dr Watson. What have they got to do with buying toothpaste at Tesco's? Nothing, but what's wrong with: 'It's *Watson* every *Holmes* bathroom shelf?' I'm sure Colgate would be pleased to hear that their products are *what's on* every *home's* bathroom shelf!

2. Hidden treasures. The high seas and pirates have no relevance here as we're talking about Ordnance Survey maps, but there's a suggestion of wealth, gems, jewels, riches. In fact, the first prize for this competition was won with: 'Their *wealth* of information *enriches* the traveller's journey and *reveals* the *jewels* of our countryside.' Very apt. The winner even introduced the word 'reveal' to counteract 'hidden' in the opening phrase.

3. Sound advice. If you can think of a piece of sound advice which is commonly phrased, and can adapt it to this slogan, that too would be an apt completion. However, I would automatically think of a music connection in this instance, perhaps introducing the names of current popular groups or singers. If you want to use that famous old pun, the Chopin Liszt (the shopping list), it will have to be in a new, inspired way. But you could point out that you can shop in 'record time', that Tesco is your 'Number One' store or that the small bill is 'music to your ears'. There are many, many ways to complete a 'sound' slogan. Start with as many relevant words as you can think of (or find in your thesaurus) and play around with them until an *idea* has become a *slogan*.

4. *Electrifying*. As with the above example, the puns on 'electric' words are almost endless. The winner of this competition said he or she was 'switched on to powerful bargains'. But other thought-inspiring or 'super-charged' words are current, shocking, socket, amp, watt and ohm: as in 'Watt *amp*le bargains for your ohm'. Has anything here made your eyes light up? Before I get carried away, let's go on to the final example.

5. *Sporting Chance*. Again, an opportunity to use 'number one', or 'track record', 'first class', 'dead eat' (dead heat) or 'winning post' or any fresh ideas that you might have on a sporting subject.

Are you getting the hang of it yet? If you have any entry forms in your possession, sit down with them and repeat this exercise. Look for any clues or suggestions which the competition organisers have given you and you'll be on your way to giving the judges what they're looking for (and so infrequently get) – aptness. I've seen a number of articles written by panellists who have said that they've read many amusing and clever (often downright weird) slogans during judging which didn't win because they made no attempt to relate to the product, the prize or the general theme of the competition, so *aptness* is an important point to consider when constructing slogans.

One excellent example of an easy-to-spot theme was the Burrough's 'Doubles' competition which appeared in the Press some months ago. Burroughs are the people who market double measures of popular spirits and mixers (gin and tonic, whisky and ginger, etc.) in individual bottles. The illustration for the competition was of a woman, looking remarkably like Ingrid Bergman, saying 'Rick, would you buy me a Burroughs Double for the chance to escape to Hollywood?' (two weeks in Hollywood being the main prize), to which a dead-ringer for Humphrey Bogart, who played the part of Rick in the film *Casablanca*, replied, 'Sure, blue eyes, because . . .' That film, or films generally, actors, Hollywood, etc. would all be themes that the judges would be looking for in the winning slogan for this particular competition.

One final tip on the subject of aptness. If the beginning of the slogan makes no distinct suggestion of a theme, as with 'I buy Brand X at Store Y because . . .', then look at the prize or prizes being offered, as another successful way of ensuring an apt slogan is by introducing a theme yourself *related* to those prizes. If, for example, the first prize is a weekend for two at a health farm, you could write about the 'slim' bills, the fact that you never 'waist' time at the check-out or the healthy aspect of the product itself. A thesaurus is an indispensable tool with 'themes' and you should be reaching for yours whenever you see the word 'apt' on competition entry forms.

Humour

My biggest 'beef' with competition organisers is when they ask for witty slogans to be completed for the most boring and ordinary products. Or, if the theme is one which can be exploited in an amusing way, they ruin the effect by only giving the comper a few extra words to play with.

That 'grouse' aside, a witty slogan, whether specifically asked for or not, is one way of attracting the judges' attention to your entry in preference to the hundreds of final efforts they might be asked to look at. Humour is a very personal thing, but I've seen some crackers from among the boring or the banal which often win major prizes. Slogans like, for a beauty product, 'I'm no Krystle in suspenders, more Dot Cotton in Eastenders.' Or the comper who carried off a deserving first prize in a cider 'dry humour' competition because she said that she was the

91

lady 'who swallowed the spider that giggled and giggled and giggled in cider.' Brilliant!

Try to inject some humour into your own slogans and, by making the judges smile, good fortune is more likely to smile on you.

Acrostics

This is the term given to a slogan constructed from the letters of a given product, which then become the first letters of the words you're using to endorse that product. It's also one way of throwing in as many adjectives as possible for good measure.

I believe that acrostics has always been more popular in the USA than it has been over here, but I've seen a number of British competitions recently which have featured this kind of slogan. Perhaps companies are following their counterparts in the USA and this is the shape of competitions to come.

For one acrostic competition recently, entrants were asked to devise an eight-word telegram for a new breakfast cereal using the letters TEAM NEWS. My own attempt was: Teamsters Eagerly Appreciate Mouthwatering Nourishment Enthusiastically Wolfing Seconds.

Flattery

Do try to be positive when writing your slogans. A judge won't want to be told you buy product X only because a rival's product is always out of stock at your local supermarket. Nor will you win first prize simply by stating that you buy the product because it's cheaper than anyone else's. If you're stumped for an idea for a slogan, then sit down and think *why* you buy that product and *expand* from there. It's not enough to say that it tastes good or lasts a long time, you must include some flattering adjectives while you're at it! After all, if you can't find at least *one* good thing to say about the product, why are you buying it in the first place?

You may think that a sincere or flattering slogan will pale in comparison with some of the witty, word-playing efforts other compers might come up with. But believe me, such slogans *have* won major prizes in the past. One large chain of jewellers (excuse the pun) awarded first prize of a holiday in the USA plus £500 spending money to the entrant who said he shopped at their stores because of the good value and courteous, knowledgeable staff!

We all like to be flattered – try buttering up the judges with some sincere expressions of your own.

Now you've had some food for thought, let's look at the best way of putting your thoughts down on paper.

I chose, at random, 50 prize-winning slogans which had won first prize in competitions in the last year or two. Of these, 34 were written in verse, albeit simple rhyming couplets. If my sample is representative of competitions as a whole, that means that on average over 60 per cent of winning slogans are written in verse. The majority of runners-up prizes were awarded to poetic slogans too.

Even if you hated poetry at school, this is a technique which gives you a better chance of winning prizes and isn't as difficult to master as you might think.

Take a look at these winning slogans:

- 'The colours are bright, the quality's right, forget the rest, they are the best'
- 'Compared to the rest they have proved caringly the best'
- 'When it comes to fizziness they mean business'
- 'They are a step in the right direction to hair care perfection'
- 'It tastes world class in cup, can or glass'

93

Impressed? Well, I'm much more impressed (and surprised) by the prizes they won – *major* prizes like cars, foreign holidays and cash. Don't you think you could produce slogans just as good, if not better than these? Get yourself a pad of paper and a pen and I'll show you how.

Firstly, think of a product which you buy regularly and write down as many reasons as you can as to why you buy it. For example:

1. Do you buy it as a *treat* for your family?
2. Does it represent good *value*?
3. Has it a wonderful *flavour*?
4. Can you *rely* on its high standards?

Now let's look at ways in which we can transform these comments into short, rhyming couplets.

1. What words can you think of that rhyme with 'treat'? If you're stuck for an idea, start with the letter 'a' and work your way through the alphabet. Did you stop at 'b'? How about using the word 'beat', as in 'This tasty treat is hard to beat'; or put more emphasis in, like this: 'This extra-special treat is impossible to beat'; or alternatively, 'It's an extra-special treat, impossible to beat'.

Try using words like 'neat' in a similar way and vary the slogan two or three times, as with the example above.

Don't forget words which are spelled differently, but still rhyme, such as 'wheat', as in 'The goodness of wheat in a tasty, filling treat'.

2. Value is a harder word with which to make a rhyme. But, then again, it doesn't have to be the *last* word in the rhyming couplet. Why not end your rhyme with 'value for all', as in 'For budgets big or small it's value for all'. I'm

sure you can do better. Have a go using the word 'value' in as many ways as you can.

3. Flavour is a useful word, as it rhymes with, among others, 'savour', 'waiver', even 'saver'. Here are a few examples to inspire you: 'More taste, more flavour – there's so much to savour'; 'It has a delicious fresh flavour from which I never waiver'; 'It's a jar full of flavour and a great money saver'.

See how you can improve upon these, then have a go at a few of your own. Perhaps you could think of a product for which you could use the word 'raver'!

4. Rely is another word which rhymes easily. How many words can you write down which rhyme with it? Did you think of, for example, buy, defy, die, satisfy and verify? What do you think of: 'On its taste you can rely, it never fails to satisfy'?

Another kind of rhyme you could try is the one where the rhyming word is second to last, the last word being the same for both lines. This can be very effective and has been used time and time again by a number of successful prize-winners. For example 'Brand A excites me, its flavour delights me' or 'Once you've tried it, you'll always buy it'.

Some of the product's attributes might present a more difficult rhyme than the examples I've given above. That's where a rhyming dictionary comes into its own. Learn to use yours and you'll never be short of a word that rhymes with what you want to say.

Remember, too, that practice makes perfect. The more you try to write slogans, the easier it will become, and by practising with simple slogans from ideas you've had yourself, you're well on the way to writing good, prize-winning slogans for the entry forms you'll already be collecting in your monthly file.

Don't worry too much about originality, wit or aptness to begin with. Just concentrate on the mechanics of constructing a simple, rhyming couplet and once you've mastered the technique, all these other factors can be incorporated later.

Why not make a habit of spending, say, 10 minutes a day writing rhymes about the products to be found in your store cupboard? Start with the words 'I buy Brand X because . . .' and see what gems you can come up with. Make sure you keep all your early efforts – you never know when they might come in useful. Even if you're less than happy with your initial slogans, they can be used as a springboard to future, more inspired ideas.

When you're confident about this exercise, you can then take the next step – choosing slightly more original, and therefore less well-worn, words which the judges are likely to come across infrequently. Words like technology, design, excellence, convenience, economic are not common, so you'll greatly increase your chances of winning by using them, or words like them, in an effective way.

One occasion when I did this was when I completed 'Batchelor's are cooking with gas because . . .' with 'the cost is economic, for cuisine gastronomique!'

When you've completed your slogan, but *before* you write it on the entry form, *read it aloud*. If it doesn't *sound* right to you, it won't to the judges and they'll inevitably read them out to themselves and each other during the judging session.

If it's a two-line verse, are there the same number of syllables on each line? Look again at my Batchelor's slogan, in which there are seven syllables in each phrase. If the scan is right, the verse will sound much better. Here's the same example, worded differently: 'The cost is economic and helps me produce cuisine gastronomique'. Too many words cluttering up the sentence have ruined the scan and also the effect of the rhyme. Just because you're allowed 10 words, you don't have to use them all. Only use sufficient words to make the verse *sound* right – make sure your verses appeal to the ear, as well as to the eye.

Sometimes you'll be asked to complete a limerick, the 'There was a young lady from Bolton . . .' type of verse. The competition may require you to add anything up to four lines of a five-line limerick in an amusing way, as the very nature of limericks makes them amusing. I'm sure you'll have seen many examples of the limerick. Edward Lear popularised them in his *Book of Nonsense* and Spike Milligan is a modern-day exponent of the art. But for those of you unsure which lines should rhyme with which, here's a guide to follow:

Lines 1 and 2   – rhyming couplet a–a
Lines 3 and 4   – rhyming couplet b–b
Line 5   – rhymes with 1 and 2 a

If you're asked to complete line 5 only, it should contain the same, or roughly the same, number of syllables as lines 1 and 2, with which it also rhymes. If the rules ask for three lines (i.e. you're to complete lines 3, 4 and 5), remember that lines 3 and 4 are much shorter than the other three, giving the limerick its distinctive, short, sharp sound.

An example of a five-line limerick would be:

There was a man from Nantucket	(a)
Who kept all his cash in a bucket	(a)
But his daughter named Nan	(b)
Ran away with a man	(b)
And as for the bucket, Nantucket	(a)

Note that there are nine syllables in each of lines 1, 2 and 5 and six in lines 3 and 4. Limericks also lend themselves well to puns or plays on words, as you can see in the second inclusion of Nantucket, in this sense meaning 'Nan took it'.

Puns/Plays on Words

I *love* puns and one of the books I adore dipping into every so often is John S. Crosbie's *The Dictionary of Puns* (Futura). It has given me inspiration on countless occasions when I've been looking for a witty completion. If it's available at your local library, or if you would like to add it to your own book-shelves, I can guarantee you much amusement from it.

Slogans which effectively use puns or clever word-play are positive 'attention grabbers' and, as that's the point of the exercise when writing competition tie-breakers, you should give some thought to trying this yourself.

Take a look at these examples:

'One is biological, the other *buyer logical*'
'Danish bacon is the *pork-you-pine-for*'
'Eating Italian *ciao* is my favourite *pasta-time*'
'I *can-na-letto* myself buy any other'
'I tried another store's shopping trolley but couldn't *budget*'

Journalists are wonderful at this sort of word-play and it's worth making a note of any you see in newspapers or magazines so you can use them when the need arises. For example, in a recent article about Australia, the writer invited readers to enjoy some Down-Under 'Oz-pitality'. In one competition for an Australian holiday which I entered (a very popular prize when the film *Crocodile Dundee* was released), I said that I would like to visit Australia so that I could 'ab-original' memories for years to come!

Have I convinced you yet that *you* could come up with a clever prize-winning slogan? No? Well, let me tell you how I solved a recent slogan problem of my own.

I decided to enter the 'Fitter not Fatter' competition promoting British-grown potatoes. I had looked through my reference books at home, and in the library, and was absolutely certain that my answers to the six questions set were 100 per cent correct. I'd bought 5 lb of King Edward's and my local greengrocer signed the entry form as 'proof of purchase'. I also had the front page of the local newspaper which was to judge the initial heats, as this was also a requirement for entry. All these items were ready to be sent to the competition address, but I was stumped for a slogan. I had to complete, in no more than 12 words, the following sentence: 'With British-grown potatoes you're fitter not fatter because . . .'

I had gone to visit a friend for coffee one morning and arrived a little early – she hadn't returned from dropping her children at school. In my handbag was the British potatoes entry form. If the slogan eluded me any longer, I wouldn't get it in before the closing date. So I used the spare 10 minutes I had, quietly sitting in my car, staring at the entry form and hoping for inspiration.

The prizes were related to sports – three first prizes of family-activity holidays worth £2,500 and £250 worth of sports activity equipment for heat prize-winners. I thought of all the different sports I could and tried to use them in a slogan. Nothing gelled. I then thought of the health aspect and how potatoes, if not liberally buttered or roasted in inches of fat, *were* tasty and low in calories. Taking this idea a step further, I thought about the major disease affecting adults in Britain – heart disease, or *heart attacks*. Now I was getting somewhere, but I wanted to include some reference to sport as well. Another word for attack could be assault, as in assault course, which I checked in my *Dictionary of Synonyms and Antonyms* when I got home. After a few, initial jottings my final slogan became: 'With British-grown potatoes you're fitter not fatter because they assault your taste-buds without attacking your heart.' Again, I can't tell you the outcome of this competition as, at time of writing, the entry date had just closed, but I was proud of my attempt – one which took a little over 10 minutes to write – and feel that, even if I don't win, it was an original slogan of a high standard.

There are many different ways in which you can introduce effective word-play into your slogans. Another example is the *contrasting* slogan, where two words or phrases of contrasting meanings are presented in one telling sentence, as in: '*Heavenly* designs at *down-to-earth* prices' or '*High* standards, *low* cost'.

Make a list of some similar 'opposites' that you could use and find something positive to say about a chosen product in order to use them in this eye-catching way.

Homonyms are words which sound the same but mean something entirely different, as in these examples: 'Our butchers are pleased to *meet* you, with *meat* to please you' or 'The perfume is heaven *scent*'. Remember Dracula's slogan – 'Love at first bite'? Well the idea is similar, with the word 'bite' being substituted for 'sight'.

Another successful way to produce eye-catching sentence completions is to take a well-known phrase or saying and relate it to the product, as in: 'You're *home and dry* with this deodorant'; 'When I clean my toilet with Brand B I'm *flushed with success*'; and 'This bacon is *streaks ahead* of all the others'.

WHERE TO LOOK FOR INSPIRATION

I hope I've given you some inspiration in this chapter, and

that by completing the exercises, particularly the one on aptness, you'll see that the majority of competitions have already given you some clues to work from. You should then find additional inspiration from your thesaurus to supplement them with other words of a similar theme. In addition, Chapter 5 has a section on 'Books for Slogans' (pages 81–3), covering many sources of inspiration which have helped me in the past.

Let me remind you again to make a note of clever word-plays used by journalists. They have to write attention-seeking headlines to convey the meaning of the underlying article, often in fewer words than those afforded to slogan tie-breakers. Don't risk losing these 'gems' on spare pieces of paper – keep them in your comping notebook (or home computer), ready for when writer's block hits you.

Likewise, advertising executives are adept at producing succinct, effective slogans to sell their clients' products. While it's not enough to 'lift' an existing advertising slogan and quote it verbatim elsewhere, the *idea* behind it might be just what you need to put you on the right track. The inspiration for one of my competition slogans was on a poster in the street. In fact, once you've learned to keep your eyes open for slogan ideas, you'll be amazed at the variety of sources in your local high street alone. Take, for example, a church close to my home which regularly has eye-catching posters outside. My favourite reads 'Love Won Another' and I'm just waiting for the opportunity to use it.

Look at 'old chestnuts' and other compers' winning slogans, by all means, as you can often find some inspiration from their efforts, but be wary of repeating them word for word as it could work to your disadvantage.

Finally, don't reject your own reasons for buying the pro-duct. If you really mean what you're writing, your sincerity will doubtless come across on paper and the judges may reject the excruciating puns in favour of your pertinent prose!

STICK TO THE RULES!

Don't be put off by thinking that your slogans will be any less worthy than those which panellists are usually called upon to judge. If you can master these simple techniques and try them out regularly on your entry forms, I think you'll be pleasantly surprised to find they win you a prize one day. When I asked one PR contact of mine how exceptional were the winning slogans he had come across, the reply was that there do tend to be a few slogans that are a cut above the rest; not a lot – *a few*. Try to ensure you're one of them and just see how many prizes come your way.

Competition directions can be misleading if you don't read them properly. Most are straightforward and you'll be asked to complete a sentence in an apt, original or witty way in a maximum of, say, 10 words. But beware the instruction which says 'complete this sentence in less than 10 words'. That doesn't mean write a 10-word slogan, it means write a maximum 9-word slogan! Make sure you don't make that mistake.

Now here are some other Do's and Don'ts to bear in mind when writing slogans:

1. Don't use the first thought that comes into your head, as it will have doubtless been the first thought of hundreds of others. My advice would be to spend whatever time you can spare 'playing' with words and ideas, but then set any final slogans aside to be looked at again in a few days' time (put them in your monthly file for safe keeping). By then fresh ideas may have sprung to mind to improve or replace your earlier work. *Originality*, a common requirement in consumer competitions, means offering something different to anyone else.

2. *Don't* try to cram too much into one sentence or you will lose the effect of what you're trying to say. The only time when an abundance of adjectives is best put to effective use is with acrostics, and even then you'll need to make sure the resulting slogan makes sense.

3. *Don't* use long and difficult words – simplicity is much more effective and the judges won't have the time or the inclination to reach for their dictionaries.

4. *Don't* be too contrived – puns can be amusing, but also excruciating.

5. *Don't* over-exaggerate – if the product is a luxury, there's no point saying you buy it because it's cheap.

6. *Don't* make your references too obscure by using catch-phrases of music-hall comedians, or the words of 'golden mouldies'.

7. *Do* be topical, by all means, but make sure it's well-known topicality.

8. *Do* play safe when using 'contractions' (i.e. words such as it's, I've or there's). I always prefer to think of these as two words for the purpose of counting the number of words used in my slogans. That's not to say that a panel of judges, faced with an outstanding slogan, wouldn't award the sender first prize even if a contraction took the number of words over the maximum allowed. But as there is no hard and fast rule about this, make sure your more modest efforts 'fit the bill'.

9. *Do* send in more than one entry if you're allowed to, as that way you'll hedge your bets by entering, say, a verse, a witty one-liner and sincere praise. But *don't* photocopy or send in multiple entries unless you're told to do so, otherwise they'll be disqualified.

CHAPTER 7

HOW TO 'QUALIFY'

WHAT ARE 'QUALIFIERS'?

Roughly half the competitions you're ever likely to enter will ask for a little more than providing a solution to a 'teaser' and writing an apt or witty slogan. You'll need, for these, to attach a 'qualifier' or 'proof-of-purchase' with your entry form.

The competition organisers might ask for a label from a tin of beans or soup, the quality-control panel from a carton of ice-cream (also known as the bar-code, this is the panel with black lines of varying thicknesses found on most products nowadays), or the top of a packet of washing powder – it varies from competition to competition.

I've known avid compers keep literally drawers full of such labels, ring-pulls, packet and bottle tops in order to be prepared for any qualifiers they might need for future competitions. This isn't a practice I indulge in, nor would I encourage you to either. After all, who really wants to keep a year's supply of grocery rubbish in case the odd label or two is asked for to qualify in a competition? More importantly, this sort of hoarding is largely a waste of time. Competition organisers will cunningly ask you to send in a specially printed label or a quantity of tokens printed on their usual labels which are then distributed only for the duration of the competition. That means that any old label won't do: you'll need to buy a special 'competition' pack or tin to qualify, so whatever you saved six months ago might as well go where it belongs – in the dustbin!

HOW TO ENSURE YOU ALWAYS HAVE THE QUALIFIERS YOU NEED

Special competition packs have a habit of disappearing from supermarket shelves very quickly, and when the next delivery of the product arrives, you'll find it's the usual label which graces it, not the one you need to complete your entry. Whenever you find an entry form which mentions sending in a qualifier or proof-of-purchase, have a good look to see immediately *how many* are required. If possible, buy the total number of qualifiers that you'll need at once. Have you ever been frustrated by having collected nine tokens and, try as you might, been unable to find that all-important tenth token to enable you to send away for a certain offer? Well, the same thing can happen with competition qualifiers. If you shop every two or three days, keep an eye on the shelves. If those special wrappers are rapidly dwindling, you can be sure that when the new stock comes in, the product will be labelled in its usual way.

If you shop only once or twice a month and the product you want to buy will keep indefinitely, perhaps, as I've suggested, you could buy as many of the special packs that you'll need to ensure that you have all the qualifiers required for a specific competition.

For example, Colgate ran a book token offer a while ago. Not a competition, I grant you, but the principle is the same. For each £5 Book Token I needed to collect ten special tokens – 2 on each large packet of Colgate toothpaste. I have learned my lesson the hard way, so I bought all five packets of toothpaste at the one time and claimed my Book Token straight away. We happen to like

Colgate toothpaste, it doesn't go 'off' and I know that, for the next few months at least, we'll never run out of it!

Get used to keeping your till receipts too. Many consumer competitions are run in conjunction with a particular supermarket chain. The supermarket wants to be sure that you'll buy the product from its store and you'll be asked to send in your till receipt, in addition to any qualifiers they might also ask for, with the price you paid clearly circled.

USING THE FILING SYSTEM TO YOUR ADVANTAGE

Of course, if you follow my advice and set up the filing system mentioned in Chapter 3, then you'll have the perfect storage place for those qualifying labels and till receipts. If you, like I used to, shove the odd label or token in a drawer, you're sure to forget about them, finding them again only when the competition closing date has passed and they're worthless. So, always put everything you need to enter each competition, along with the entry form, in the relevant monthly file.

If you're at all worried about lots of labels, bottle tops or till receipts lying loosely in your monthly file (perhaps you've got a busy month of competitions ahead and it's already full of paper?), then do what I do occasionally. If, as with the dog food competition I entered some months ago, I have five or six labels to send in for one competition, I keep them all together in a clearly marked envelope – an already-used one will do. This keeps your file tidier, so you're even less likely to lose a valuable qualifier.

Some competition rules ask you, quite clearly, to attach the qualifier to the entry form. This is a sensible idea as it prevents the two coming adrift at the handling house, so they don't know if you've really sent one in or not. I usually attach paper qualifiers, till receipts and entry forms together with a stapler, but Sellotape works just as well – glue is a bit too messy. However, be on the look-out for rules which clearly state that qualifiers should *not* be attached to the entry form. Why competition organisers should ask this is a mystery to me, as I would have thought it made their job more difficult for the reasons I've given above. But if that's one of the rules, make sure you obey it.

I'm glad to see that competition organisers are now being much more sensible in their requests for qualifiers. Past requests for the complete packaging of their products meant extra expense in postage, and envelopes coming apart in the post, whereas a specified section of that packaging would have been sufficient for ensuring that the entrant bought the product in the first place. If you're asked for bottle tops as qualifiers, crush them with a hammer first to flatten them. Labels stuck to plastic bottles are best soaked off and then laid on kitchen roll to dry out. If you're asked for a complete box or packet, see what you can cut off to make the qualifier still acceptable to the promoter, but easier to get through the post.

Sometimes promoters completely miss the fact that two identical packet flaps are featured on one packet and that by asking for only one of these as a qualifier, the comper has *two* chances for entry. I've used this way of increasing my entries – and therefore my chances – in the past, so should you.

CHAPTER 8

THE GOLDEN RULES

TWELVE DO'S AND DON'TS FOR SUCCESSFUL COMPING

1. When you spot competition forms on supermarket shelves or wherever, don't just take one – if possible, take two or three. The rules may allow you to make more than one entry, which is always worth doing as it increases your chances of winning. Remember what I've already said about your slogans – if you can send in multiple entries, then try a variety of different slogans: witty, rhyming, sincere, etc. You never know exactly what a judge is looking for in a slogan, so it's always best to hedge your bets and offer him or her as wide a choice as possible.

The other advantage of taking a few entry forms at a time is that if you spoil the first one in any way (see point 2 below), you've always got a spare one handy. Of course, when entry forms appear in magazines or newspapers, you're unlikely to want to buy two or three copies of the same issue, so you'll have to be extra careful not to mess up these forms. But perhaps a friend also gets that publication and is not an avid comper. It's worth asking if you might have their form too.

2. Don't complete your entry forms in ink until you are 100 per cent confident that you're happy with the answers you've given and the slogan that you've thought of.

I've made the mistake of writing a slogan on an entry form, in ink, anxious to put it down on paper, only to find that I have been 'inspired' a day or so later with an even better one. And do you think I could find another entry form for the same competition? No! So write in your notebook first, or on the entry form in pencil if you have to. Only fill in with pen when you are completely happy with what you've written. Remember, most competition rules include the one which states 'Entries altered (or illegible) will be disqualified.'

3. Never miss a closing date. Always make sure you keep your competitions in some sort of date order, even if you decide not to try my filing system. If a competition closes on 30 August and you don't spot it until 2 September, you've missed a valuable chance to become a winner. I'm an optimist but, believe me, no competition organiser will look at an entry form received after the closing date. There's usually a rule to this effect in every competition you'll ever enter. Don't waste your time and money sending in an out-of-date competition. Just make sure you don't make the same mistake twice.

On the subject of closing dates, aim to send off your entry forms *at least* one week before the closing date. If it's a competition that closes on 31 July, then the latest date by which you should have posted it would be 24 July. I always put first-class stamps on entries I've posted in this way, regardless of the Post Office's assurances that first-class mail will arrive at its destination the next working day. If, however, I've found the answers and slogan quickly, or perhaps have completed a free prize-draw coupon requiring nothing more than a name and address, and I've two or three weeks before the competition's closing date, I save money by using a second-class stamp.

My local newspaper is always running competitions and

I've picked up a lot of useful, small prizes through entering them. Their offices are only two miles away from my home and I pass them regularly when visiting a friend. So I always make a point of posting entries for their competitions by hand – no stamp required. Don't think you're at a disadvantage when doing this: I've certainly not found that to be the case. In fact, it has proved to be extremely useful when the closing date is only a few days after I receive that particular newspaper.

Here's another tip – a few competitions I've come across allow you to send in your entries 'Freepost'. That means exactly what it says and those competitions don't even cost you the price of a stamp.

4. *Never* be tempted to send off competitions under anyone else's name – even with a friend or relative's permission. Competition organisers frown upon this practice and may even retract the prize if they find out.

In any case, it would be just your luck to win a luxury cruise for two in Auntie Maud's name where you'd be in no position to insist that you and your spouse go instead. After all, if the competition is entered in Auntie Maud's name then *she* is the one who is legally entitled to the prize.

5. *Don't* rely on unsubstantiated answers. If Uncle Jack insists he knows who scored the winning goal in the 1970 World Cup Final, *fine*. But it's easy enough to check that he's right. If you don't get the questions 100 per cent correct, then you'll not win, no matter how good your slogan is! In question-and-answer competitions, the slogan is generally a tie-breaker, which means that it's only considered when deciding the prize-winners among those entries with correct answers. There's only one occasion when you should ignore this rule and that's when you've tried every source you can think of and you're *still* short of an answer to one question. Well, in this situation, if you're

sure that the answer cannot be found, then make a calculated guess – especially if it's a multiple-choice question and you're given two or three answers to choose from.

For one competition I entered, I had to give the location of the first lending library in Britain. Try as I might, I was unable to discover any reference to this anywhere. My father suggested that the industrialist Andrew Carnegie was responsible for the founding of many libraries. I looked again at the entry form. There were three cities from which I could make my choice – London, Birmingham or Edinburgh. Andrew Carnegie was a Scot by birth, so I guessed at Edinburgh and, after receiving a copy of the correct solution, found that I was right!

Don't forget, if you don't enter you can't win. As a last resort, *guess*. At worst, you've lost the price of a stamp. At best, your calculated guess could pay off and *win*.

6. If slogans are your stumbling-block, keep trying. Believe me, the more you write them, the easier they'll become. Writer's block happens even to professional writers – authors whose books sell in thousands and yet who can sit at a typewriter one day and think of nothing to put on that piece of paper.

If you're at a loss for a particular slogan, don't worry about it. If you're using my filing system, you'll have up to three weeks in which to come up with an idea.

I needed a slogan for a competition run by a company offering Brut gift packs as prizes (very useful for a Christmas present, I thought). The slogan I had to complete referred to the Brut girl who 'feels like a new man'. I thought about this one for a few days but no ideas came to me. Later, I was walking down the high street when I saw a sign in a shop window, saying 'We've got the gift for it'. That started me thinking about the Brut slogan

111

I needed. Immediately I thought of 'gift' (i.e. the prize offered), then the words 'sense of smell' came to me (i.e. the smell of the product), then finally a play on the word 'odour' (as Brut also make deodorants). My final slogan became: 'Brut makes her feel like a new man because she's got the gift for sensing when it's all 'odour'.' Sorry, though, I can't tell you how I got on with this competition as, at time of writing, the results haven't been announced.

Even if, after days of thinking of ideas and looking for inspiration, you can think of nothing other than the most banal slogan, enter it. Banal slogans *have* won prizes before. In fact, on a number of occasions, the winning slogans have been so banal that I've wondered if my brilliant ones have gone over the heads of the competition organisers! It all depends on how many entries there are, how many correct answers are received and what appeals to a certain set of judges. *Never* fail to send in an entry form just because you're less than happy with your slogan.

7. *Consider* how much the competition will cost you to enter against the value of the prizes offered. I'm not trying to encourage you to spend all your housekeeping money on products you would never normally buy or use, but what I am saying is that *occasionally* a super competition comes to light which is worth entering, even if it's a product you rarely buy.

I don't own a dog, but recently two large dog-food companies ran competitions with money prizes of £50,000. To enter I needed a number of labels from their cans, costing me less than £1.50 for each competition. I decided to buy the cans, take off the labels, then give them to a grateful, dog-owning friend. There was nothing in the rules saying the winner *had* to own a dog and my friend promised to loan her 'best friend' to me should I be lucky enough to win and need a dog for publicity pictures! I considered that it was worth such a small outlay for the possibility of winning such a large sum of money. Certainly think about it, but remember the word I've used above – occasionally – and only if the prize is *really* big.

Actually, this story has rather an amusing ending. No, I didn't win the £50,000 (perhaps if I had owned a dog I might have stood a better chance, I don't know), but I did receive a runners-up prize: a book telling me everything you need to know about owning and raising – you've guessed it – a dog! My husband detests pets of any description, so we're unlikely ever to need the book. Still, it could be a useful Christmas present for someone.

Finally, one word of caution. If you remove the labels from tins of food *before* you're ready to open them, mark exactly what's in them with black, indelible pen. I'm sure mine isn't the first husband to have sampled a can of unlabelled dog food thinking it was beef stew!

8. *Do* keep a note of the competitions you've entered, together with the answers to the questions and your slogans, in a notebook as I've suggested before. It's amazing how useful this can be in the future. If I've a spare, duplicate entry form (or, alternatively, a photocopy of the entry form), I stick that into my notebook. Having spent a lot of time researching my answers, I note them down in case the same question pops up again somewhere else.

My slogans are too important for me to forget about, even ones that don't win can be improved upon. I write each of them down on the appropriate page, noting the total number of words I had to use, together with whether the slogan was meant to be witty, apt or whatever. As I've said before, but it's worth saying over and over again, you can often adapt an already used slogan. If that slogan was a winner for you once, it's certainly worth changing slightly and using it again. Even if it wasn't, who knows? It might appeal to a different judge next time.

I would also suggest you send away for the competition results in order to receive the actual answers, the correct order-of-merits and to see what the winning slogans were. If you subscribe to *Competitors Companion, Competitor's Journal* or Enter-Prize, you'll find some of the winning slogans published by them in future months. And, of course, you can always buy booklets containing nothing but prize-winning slogans. I've already expressed my opinions on using old chestnuts (see Chapter 6), so I'll leave it up to you whether you rely on these, or your own, original thoughts when submitting slogans for consumer competitions.

9. *Always* fill in your entry forms in *block capitals*, even if the rules don't actually ask you to do this. One rule that crops up again and again in competitions is the one that asks you to make your entry *legible*.

Remember, competition organisers often have hundreds if not thousands of entries to look at before deciding upon the winner. If they can't read your writing, don't kid yourself that they're going to sit down and spend time trying to work out what you've written – they won't. You'll be disqualified just as simply as if you had spilled your coffee all over the entry form (make sure you never do this, either). Judges are looking for clean, easy-to-read entries, as well as wonderful answers and brilliant slogans. You might think your handwriting is easily legible, but don't chance it. Get the judges on your side and write in block capitals every time. It'll soon become second nature to you.

10. *Don't* forget to put your name and address on your entries. No, I'm not treating you like an idiot – you'd be surprised at how many people, even regular compers, fail

to do this once in a while. They get so excited about their correct answers and prize-winning slogans that off goes the entry form and, even if they would have won, no one knows where to send the prize!

The easiest competition in which to forget this rule is the one that has no entry form, but asks you to put your answers on a plain piece of paper or postcard. I always make a point of writing my name and address (in block capitals, of course) *first*.

Maybe you've got some of those sticky labels with your name and address already printed on: use them by all means. The competition organisers won't mind, in fact they're grateful for easily read particulars. It makes their job easier and there's less chance of your prize going astray in the post.

11. *Don't* forget, either, to include whatever qualifiers you're asked for. They form part of the rules of the competition and your entry will not be considered if you don't include exactly what's asked for. If your filing system is as good as mine, you should have no difficulty in extracting the right number of labels, till receipts, etc., along with the relevant entry form.

12. *Don't* get despondent. Enjoy comping for what it is:
- A chance to have some fun
- A way of increasing your knowledge
- An absorbing and interesting hobby

If you enter at least half-a-dozen competitions regularly (and that means *every month*), do your best to get the answers right, and can put together a simple, rhyming couplet, it's also a golden opportunity to win some valuable prizes for *free*.

I'm still waiting for a big win since having my new kitchen installed in early 1987, but there has not been a single month since then when I haven't won a prize, no matter how small. I've had my hair coloured for free, used beauty products I received for free, use a camera that cost me nothing, spent a wonderful anniversary evening at a top restaurant for free – I could go on for pages more. In fact, I very often send Christmas or birthday presents (prizes I don't want myself) which cost me absolutely nothing.

No one can expect to win a car every month, or a cruise or luxury holiday (who could manage to get away that often, anyway?). Again, you have to consider the odds. There's only one *first* prize in most competitions you'll enter, but often 10 or even more runners-up prizes, so your chance of winning one of those is greater. I would much rather have the excitement of regular, small prizes coming through my door than wait 12 months (or even longer) before that single, major prize comes my way.

That's not to say that one day a really super first prize won't be yours – because I'm sure it will. But, in the meantime, your new hobby will certainly give you something to tell your friends!

COMPETITION RULES – OK?

As I've said repeatedly before (but it's so important that I don't mind doing so again), it's *essential* that you follow the rules set by the competition organisers. They're always worth reading because each competition will have its own, unique set of rules and all your good work finding answers and writing slogans will go to waste if you're disqualified because you've not followed the correct procedure.

These are not just my own interpretations of the most common rules you are ever likely to come across, but include advice given to me by the people who should know – the competition organisers themselves. They're in no particular order and will never all relate to one competition, although each rule has been specified by an organiser for a competition I've entered in the past year.

1. *The judges' decision is final and legally binding and no correspondence will be entered into.* This means, don't bother to write in if you don't win, even if you feel the tie-breaker which won wasn't nearly as good as your own. It's the *judges'* decision that counts.

Well, who are the judges, you might ask? I must admit that I've never been one myself, although this would be an interesting experience for the future (competition organisers please note), but from the enquiries I've made about them, I can tell you something about who they're likely to be, their role and that of the 'handling house'.

As you might expect, an odd number of judges is the most sensible, as this avoids the situation where two might prefer one entry and two another. The actual number will depend upon the company or companies involved and the expected size of entry, but five would seem to be the average. Of these, only one is required, under the Code of Practice of the Advertising Standards Authority, to be 'independent' (i.e. not belong to either the company which is promoting the competition or their agents, the advertising agency or PR company). A likely panel of judges would be the sales manager or sales promotion manager of the company involved in the competition; the brand manager or product manager responsible for the product; an advertising executive from the advertising agency or an executive from the PR company; a 'professional' person with whom the company has some connection or someone experienced in the field of comping (perhaps someone who regularly contributes to a publication like *Competitors Journal*); and possibly a local or minor celebrity. Unless it's a major competition which

117

hopes to attract a large amount of national publicity, well-known TV or radio personalities come too expensive. As I've said, it's up to the company involved to choose its own panel, but if you're interested in checking out the names and occupations of the judges yourself, you can always send an sae to those contests which publish this information, along with the results, once the closing date has passed.

I've previously mentioned the 'handling house' and some of you may be in the dark as to what this actually refers to. The handling house is the central point to which all entries are sent, although not all companies will use one when organising a competition. As you become familiar with competition addresses, you'll notice that the same ones crop up again and again – those of handling houses. They do exactly what their name implies – 'handle' competition entry forms for companies who don't want their mailrooms inundated with thousands of entries.

The brief of the handling house will vary from competition to competition; it all depends on what the companies involved want. They may be asked to forward all entries which comply with the competition rules (i.e. only 'weeding out' those entries which are disqualified for one reason or another) or, if the entry is larger, they will only forward those entries which have successfully completed the first part of the competition, leaving the tie-breakers to be judged by the panellists. However, if the competition entry is very large, and in order to give the judges a manageable number of tie-breakers from which to make their choice, the handling house may also be asked to eliminate the less creditable ones. So, in order to ensure that *your* tie-breakers are always judged by the *judges*, make sure that you follow my tips on slogan-writing in Chapter 6.

In order to ensure anonymity and fairness in handling entries, one widely used practice is for all the tie-breakers to be typed up on sheets of paper and numbered in such a way that the judges need only refer to those numbers when expressing their preference or dislike of a particular tie-breaker. Only when the final decision has been reached will the winning number or numbers be linked up with the name and address of the entrant, so that no claim of favouritism can be levelled at the judges.

2. *Entries will only be accepted on the official entry form.* Don't make plain paper entries unless you're specifically directed to do so, otherwise your efforts will be consigned to the waste-paper bin. The rules about photocopies are less well defined: sometimes they're allowed, sometimes not. I always work on the principle that if you are *not* told that you can send in photocopies of the entry forms, *don't*. If the organisers meant you to use photocopies, they would probably have told you.

3. *The company will not accept responsibility for entries lost or delayed in the post, or illegible entries.* Post early, trust that the Post Office will deliver it intact, and *always* write in capital letters.

4. *Entries must be accompanied by the correct number of proofs of purchase/qualifiers.* See Chapter 7 on qualifiers. Don't forget to put them in the envelope!

5. *Entrants must be over 18 years of age.* Sorry, under-age compers, but please don't lie about your age – it would be just your luck to win and have your prize taken away from you. Still, you could always persuade your mum or dad to enter instead.

119

6. *No third-party applications.* Don't submit an entry on behalf of your mother or Aunt Ethel (see my comments on page 110).

7. *Entries will be confined to one per household/person.* If this point is stated in the rules, you can rest assured that the company will have some means of weeding out multiple applications. There are so many competitions where these are acceptable, why risk having your efforts disqualified by breaking this rule?

8. *Winners must be prepared to accept their prizes in person and be willing to have their names published.* This rule means that the company will expect the winner to agree to some publicity and is covering itself by writing this into the rules. Whether they would go as far as to disqualify a winner who subsequently refused publicity is up to them. While the amount of publicity required will vary from company to company, I've been told that most simply require nothing more onerous than a presentation picture and a feature in the local Press. However, if you're unable or unwilling to acquiesce to this, then perhaps you should give this competition a miss.

9. *Employees of the company, their agents and their families are not eligible to enter.* If your Uncle Ray works for the company running the competition, don't embarrass him by entering this one – there are literally thousands of others with which you'll have no such connection: enter them instead.

10. *No alternative prizes. No cash alternative.* The prizes are as stated and cannot be exchanged for cash – so don't bother to ask. However, this doesn't stop you selling your

unwanted prize privately if it's a readily-saleable item, such as a car.

But, if you really don't have room in your kitchen for the appliance being offered, or if the holiday you're trying to win has to be taken on specific dates and coincides with an important family occasion, consider whether it really is worth your while entering. For example, one competition recently had a trip to Lapland for two adults as its prize. In the rules it stated that the flight would take place on 19 December, to return on 22 December. No variation in those flight dates was possible and no cash alternative was offered. It's my young daughter's birthday on 19 December and I really didn't want to be flying out to Lapland on that day, so I didn't bother to enter that competition.

Similarly, as my two children are so young, and as I have no one who could look after them for two weeks at a time, I avoid competitions with holiday prizes for two adults only. There are many holidays to be won for families (e.g. trips to DisneyWorld, Legoland, etc.), and I know in my heart of hearts that I would enjoy winning one of these rather than wondering if all is well at home while I'm sunning myself in the Bahamas. The time to enter these competitions, for me, will be when the children are old enough to look after themselves. So, always consider whether the prize on offer will suit your circumstances. If not, why not leave that chance for someone else? Believe me, there are thousands of competitions to suit us all.

11. *Winners will be notified no later than six weeks after the closing date.* If you haven't heard by then – better luck next time! However, if you're interested in who did win (and, more importantly, *how*), then you're usually invited to send an sae to the competition address after the closing date to receive a list of judges, winners and winning slogans. And

if you did win, particularly if it's a runners-up prize, be prepared for a long wait. I've received prizes *six months* after the competition closing date.

12. No entrant may win more than one prize/Only one prize awarded per household. You or your family may have swept the board with your multiple entries, but in fairness to others you'll only get one prize.

13. Holiday prizes must be taken when specified. If you can't get time off at the time when the holiday is offered, is it worth entering this one? (See also my comments in point 10 above.)

14. Entry implies acceptance of these rules. This means exactly what it says, so it pays to read and understand exactly what the rules are.

15. Entries will not be returned. Make a note of that superb slogan – the company won't send it back to you.

16. In the event of a tie, competitors will be asked to enter a further tie-breaking competition. With factual competitions or ones which don't rely on the personal preferences of the judges, there may be the occasion when more than one entrant meet all the criteria of the competition and it's therefore impossible to decide that one merits greater consideration than another. I'll give you an example. Say the competition asks you to answer 10 questions about the Orient Express and then requires you to estimate how long a certain journey takes. If you, along with five others, submit an all-correct entry, it would be impossible to decide which of the six of you should receive first prize, unless a draw for first prize had been written into the rules.

If the organisers are faced with six possible winners for one prize, they'll need to bring in some tie-breaker to eliminate five of those winners. The most decisive way to do this would be to then ask the six finalists to submit a slogan.

CHAPTER 9

'OUT-TAKES'

Here's a collection of stories and anecdotes about my own winning experiences which I haven't covered elsewhere in this book. I hope they go some way to showing you what fun comping can be. When you become a 'professional' comper, you'll never be short of a story to tell at parties!

THE BABY BOX

In my early days of comping, I would enter competitions I came across quite indiscriminately, regardless of whether I wanted the prize or not. One example of this was when I entered a free draw at my local supermarket for a box of baby products. Now, I have two children – Graeme and Caroline – and love them as I do, I certainly don't want any more babies. But whose name should be drawn out of the hat but mine? I duly collected a big, red box containing a month's supply of disposable nappies, bath foam, baby lotions and creams, cotton buds and all sorts of literature and money-off coupons – all related to babies.

Feeling that I should share my good fortune with someone less well-off than myself, I took the baby box to my local vicar who astounded me by saying no, he didn't know of anyone who needed this gift, but perhaps I should consider having another baby myself in order to use the products!

I'm still not sure whether that last comment was meant to be a joke or not!

CROYDON ADVERTISER TREASURE TRAIL

Our local newspaper ran a weekly 'Treasure Trail' over a number of weeks where you had to find miniature 'treasure chests' hidden in its pages, and complete a form with the relevant page numbers.

After a couple of weeks' entering, I was delighted to receive a phone call congratulating me on winning a Polaroid camera. I knew that some competition organisers don't allow one person to win more than one prize, so I suggested to my husband that, as I'd won already, he might like to fill in the competition form from then on, although he wouldn't go so far as to find the hidden 'chests' himself! What a surprise to get a second phone call a week later congratulating *Mr* Simpson on winning his wife a solid gold neckchain!

THE CYCLING COMPETITION

Saturday mornings always seem to be my best time for receiving congratulatory letters. On one Saturday I was opening my mail when, among the letters, was one from a PR company. They congratulated me on winning a runners-up prize in the Rowntree's/Forbuoy's Cycle Safety Competition, but omitted to tell me what the prize was. I would be hearing, they told me, from Rowntree's in the future and my prize forwarded to me.

I hate surprises: it's for this reason that I always keep my comping notebook up to date. I had a mental picture of the wonderful ladies' cycle that I had won, which would soon be taking me to the shops and back. Or perhaps it would be a child's bike – just in time for my daughter's birthday.

I leafed impatiently through my notebook, anxious to find out what this marvellous prize would be. And there it was in stark, black letters. The first prize was the bicycle, while the runners-up prizes were – wait for it – cycle vests! All I need to do now is to win the bicycle so that I can wear mine.

THE KNITTING-MACHINE

I've always wanted a knitting-machine but, as I've so many other hobbies and activites, and very little extra space in which to indulge in any more, my husband told me that I couldn't buy one. Not to be outdone, when I saw a competition to win a beginners' knitting-machine in a women's fiction magazine, I decided to have a go at winning one. The first prize was both a knitting-machine and a steam-press, the second was the steam-press only and the third was the knitting-machine. As I posted my entry form, I remember thinking that I wouldn't want to win second prize (there's optimism for you) as I could see little personal use for a steam-press.

When the congratulatory letter arrived from Knitmaster, I was told that I'd won – you've guessed it – the second prize, the steam-press. Foiled again! Nevertheless, my motto is, 'If you don't ask, you don't receive', so I somewhat sheepishly telephoned the company concerned, thanked them profusely for the prize but asked the lady I spoke to whether it would be possible to substitute the knitting-machine for the steam-press that I'd won. She replied that she didn't think there would be any problem about that but said that the company wouldn't be able to give me the difference between the value of the two prizes.

Not thinking that this was much anyway, I told her that this didn't matter and have been delighted ever since with my easy-to-operate knitting-machine.

It was only when I turned out the magazine in which I'd seen the competition originally, that my jaw dropped. The knitting-machine had a value of £125, while the steam-press would have cost over £300 in the shops. If I'd had my wits about me, I could have sold the steam-press, bought the knitting-machine and still have money left over. Oh well, easy come, easy go!

ANNIVERSARIES AND BIRTHDAYS

A few weeks before our seventh wedding anniversary, I was the delighted recipient of a voucher for a free champagne dinner for two at La Bonne Auberge, a wonderful restaurant in South Godstone, Surrey, serving French cuisine. My husband was delighted to find the perfect venue for our celebratory meal and even more pleased that the evening wouldn't cost him anything.

As I joke, I informed him in mid-October that, as I was unlikely to repeat such a win for my birthday on 1 November, he would have to spend his own money on me then. But what should arrive through the post a week later but vouchers to buy tickets to a West End show of our choice – and as my birthday treat I'd asked my husband to take me to the theatre!
[HAPPY COMPING!]

127